MARK WINKLER

My Daughter's KEEPER

D1260238

MY DAUGHTER'S KEEPER:

-Inspired by true events-

By Mark Winkler

Journey
Press

AN IMPRINT OF SOLEMESS MEDIA PUBLISHING

Journey Press, Chicago IL.

Copyright © 2018 Mark R. Winkler

All rights reserved. No part of this publication may be reproduced, distributed, or transmitted in any form or by any means, including photocopying, recording, or other electronic or mechanical methods, without the prior written permission of the publisher, except in the case of brief quotations embodied in critical reviews and certain other noncommercial uses permitted by copyright law. For permission requests, write to the publisher, addressed "Attention: Permissions Coordinator," at the email address below.

November Media Publishing info@novembermediapublishing.com

Ordering Information: Special discounts are available on quantity purchases by corporations, associations, and others. For details, contact the publisher at the email address above.

Printed in the United States of America

Produced & Published by November Media Publishing

Cover Illustrations Alonzo Adams

ISBN: 978-978-1-7337724-3-3 (Print Copy)

First Edition : June 2019

10 9 8 7 6 5 4 3 2 1

To all the fathers out there going through this journey, I say with humility and respect, Struggle Forth with Love!

And to my beautiful daughter. Daddy loves you very much Little Cita.

CONTENTS

ACKNOWLEDGMENTS

I would like to start by thanking my loving mother, Sandra Benson, and my father, Mel Winkler. They taught me about love, hardship, compassion, and resilience and how to be the parent I am today.

I would also like to thank my beautiful wife and best friend. Without her, this book would never have been written. She helped me find and believe once more in my inner strength and courage, which I'd hidden within my fears and doubts. She also spent many sleepless nights listening to me talk about what I should or should not add into this book and editing the first, second, and third drafts. She is my rock.

Lastly, I would like to thank my publishing team led by the wonderfully talented Tiheasha Beasley. I would like to sincerely thank Tiheasha for believing that this book needed to be shared.

If I missed your name, please charge that omission to my head and not my heart. You know I love and appreciate you.

Thank you!

FOREWORD

By Thea Monyee, LMFT/Author:

He became my David.

I had a front row seat to his metamorphosis, and it was so spectacular that I knew I had to marry him. How could I not? I watched him voluntarily walk through fire for the love of his daughter, and come out on the other side with a renewed passion for helping others.

What manner of man?

The journey you are about to share with this author is flawed, vulnerable, and tender. Many of the lessons he shares cost buckets of tears and several sleepless nights, yet, he offers it to the reader with love, centeredness, and hope. We walk into his choices, into his fears, and even into the courtroom with him, attached by our shared experiences. We see ourselves in his mistakes and recognize our reflection in his work to stay clear about who he is, and what drives him.

As a therapist, I have worked with numerous families in pain. Parents of all forms can find themselves in this story and feel supported and empowered to create their own ending. The struggle of parenting while growing is a story we often tend to keep to ourselves out of shame and guilt. Winkler liberates parents to stand in their truth and encourages decision making to come from a place of love and honesty, by telling his story with authenticity.

My advice is to cry when you feel like crying. Laugh where you feel like laughing. Heal when something pricks your heart, and then teach your children to do the same.

Happy Reading!

PROLOGUE

I didn't win. Despite what many have said, I didn't win. Getting full custody of my daughter wasn't a win or a victory. It was the result of a long, hard fight with a great deal of support from family and friends, and a tremendous amount of radical self-evaluation. My journey towards full custody started before I filed court papers asking for shared custody; it started before the sheriff knocked on my door at six a.m. to serve me with a restraining order, forbidding me to come near my child's mother and my child; it started before the Office of Child and Family Services contacted me to discuss allegations that my then-girlfriend, now my wife, had physically abused my daughter. It started with the decisions I had made in romantic relationships throughout my adult life. It started with my lack of emotional intelligence, my unwillingness to be accountable and engage in self-discipline, and my lack of self-worth.

My journey isn't unique. Many have shared similar circumstances. It is my hope that sharing my journey with you will either help you to find your path to healing sooner or act as a wake-up call before you make similar mistakes. May we all find our way back to our whole, loving selves.

CHAPTER ONE

THE SAVIOR COMPLEX

Imet my child's mother, Katherine, in 2008. It was at the tail end of a four-year stint as a sports agent for a prominent agency, and I was married. My then-wife, Stacy, whom I'd met while living in DC, was a beautiful woman with an honest heart and a warm smile that would rival the most beautiful sunset. But she struggled with chronic depression. I could see evidence of this depression . . . sadness layered in her soft eyes. I'm not judging her; I'm stating a fact, a fact I knew before we were married. I thought I could save her. I thought I could rescue her from something I knew nothing about. I thought my love was enough to heal what was "hurt and broken," and somehow magically do what years of talk and prescription therapy had failed to accomplish. What I neglected to acknowledge was that even though my wife was a good woman and deserved a good life, she was not a damsel in distress looking for a savior.

I made the deluded choice to "save" her by becoming her knight in shining armor anyway. Of course, I failed miserably. The only thing I accomplished was that I accelerated my insecurities and elevated my tendency towards stronger codependent behavior. In short, I had developed a relationship addiction that affected my ability to have a healthy, mutually satisfying relationship. This dependency made me want to be a savior, not a boyfriend or husband. With Stacy, it wasn't long before my savior complex morphed into distrustful behavior. I would question her about where she was and if she was taking her prescribed medication and going to her therapy sessions—but I never left her even after I discovered she was in fact not doing either. She had instead begun self-medicating with alcohol.

Despite this, I stayed and became unhappy in the process. I coped by cheating and justified my extramarital affairs by saying I was deeply hurt that my wife wouldn't choose me over her depression. My unhappiness—and hers too, I assumed—increased. But I could not leave her. I felt too guilty. I arrogantly thought that if I left, she would fall deeper into her depression, and her drinking would increase. I wanted—needed—a safe escape route, one that would maintain my "good guy" image and simultaneously relieve me from my unsolicited savior role.

When my long-term friend Jonathan established a managerial relationship with a rising basketball star and asked me to join his newly formed management team and move to New York to help build the company, I found that exit door. I packed up my philandering behavior and codependent thinking and moved to the Big Apple without hesitation. Stacy and I agreed that I'd go first and get things stabilized, and she'd move to New York after. The initial stabilizing period was supposed to last three to four weeks, but it lasted ten months—not because it logistically took that long but because I was enjoying my newfound life as a "single" married man. I rationalized my actions by blaming her continued failure to properly treat her depression. I was like Warren Beatty in *Bugsy*. I'd call her every night and tell her I was working on bringing her out, but I was busy enjoying all the fringe benefits of my association with the ball player, who at the time was rising in public stature. My life was golden, and I was basking in all its unsavory light.

Before too long, I was a full-fledged member of the glamorous New York social scene, with many new "friends" and several casual romantic relationships under my deceitful belt. I offered these women the same old story: I was married, but my wife and I were separated. I told that story so often, I started to believe it. I was like the father from that brilliant book *Big Fish*, who told so many tall tales about his life, he eventually became the story. When I think back on it now, I wasn't sure if the women believed my lies or not, but they rarely if ever challenged the validity of my tall tale.

It was not long before the ten months had passed. I could not delay Stacy's New York move any longer. She was headed for the Big Apple.

When I picked up Stacy from the airport, I was surprised—surprised because I was so eager to see her, and she looked peaceful. Her eyes spoke of a person free of life's burdens, free of any signs of depression and drinking. I didn't have the courage to ask her if she had been faithfully taking her medication and seeing her therapist. I wanted to, but I chose to believe she was. I chose to believe our period of separation had given her time to decide what was most important to her: our relationship. I chose to believe once again that I was her savior.

The next day, I reached out to the women I was still seeing, including Temira, whom I'd begun to have a more serious relationship with, and told them I was going to mend matters with my wife and start anew. All seemed to take the news in stride. Most of their concerns were that I'd still look out for them when it came to gaining access to key industry parties—all but one, Temira. Through my duplicitous actions, I'd led Temira to believe we were headed towards something more substantial. The truth was we were not. I knew I was still married, and even though matters with Stacy were very shaky, a part of me knew I was not prepared to leave her at that time. That was the codependent side of me. When I finally revealed this to Temira, she used many coarse words to describe me that day. I took the expletives in stride. I said that she was upset, and these harsh words were par for the course. However, the thing Temira said that hurt the most was, "I thought you were different, but you are no different from all the other lying bastards." Those words wounded the most because I had presented myself as a *good guy*, a good guy who had come to believe his lies were not so much lies but more justified extensions of reality. Temira's words indeed stung, but not enough to make me stop and do some serious self-examination.

It wasn't long before I discovered Stacy had not been seeing her therapist or taking her meds back in DC. Her depression symptoms had reemerged, and when I asked her about finding a new therapist out here and renewing her medication prescription, she refused. She said that she no longer needed either and had cured herself back in DC by leaving all the negative thinking there before coming out to New York. I wanted to believe that was true because for a while it seemed that way. However, when Stacy started isolating herself and crying profusely without apparent cause, I realized that her depression had not gone away. Additionally, I started seeing the signs of her drinking again. She would get very angry when she drank.

Stacy was able to mask all these signs only for a moment. I knew what I had to do. I dusted off my ol' trusted savior cape. I reverted to my codependent behavior of constantly trying to convince her to seek treatment. I started leaving pamphlets around the apartment about the benefits of therapy and the usefulness of medication in the treatment of depression. I also started to leave AA literature in the car so when she went for a ride, she would eventually see it. When all these passive-aggressive actions failed, I belittled her for not loving herself or us enough to seek proper help. This of course did not work either. It only frustrated her and reignited my insecurities.

During this time, I reactivated my extramarital activities. Again I justified this behavior by saying I was hurt, and this was my way of soothing the pain without abandoning my wife in her hour of need. This behavior led me to my daughter's mother, Katherine.

CHAPTER TWO

WHEN THE BOUGH BREAKS

I was attending a celebrity charity basketball game. I was going to skip the event, but I didn't feel like staying at home because I knew eventually I'd direct my attention towards Stacy in a negative way. So I went to the game. I wasn't particularly interested in meeting anyone new that night. I was just planning on having a cool night out with Jonathan, who joined me at the event. But I noticed her. She was tall and slender, with long brown hair and a cocoa complexion.

She was standing alone at the refreshment stand, so I offered to buy her a glass of wine. We sat down at a nearby table and struck up a conversation. I don't recall what we talked about, but I remember her placing her hand on mine during the conversation. At the time, it didn't seem like a big deal. I thought maybe she was a touchy-feely type of person. Maybe, I thought, I'd get *lucky* that night. I was rather buzzed. I didn't get lucky, but she did give me her number. I wouldn't call her for another three or four weeks.

When I finally called Katherine, it wasn't because I wanted to explore something meaningful. I was leaving another event, and I didn't want to go directly home. We didn't engage in sexual activity that night. We instead talked a long while. I can't recall our exact conversation; however, she later told me I seemed disconnected, and I didn't remove my sunglasses the entire time I was at her house. What she didn't know was my sunglasses were my signature "New York look."

Those glasses were my way of looking cool and allowed me to not look people directly in their eyes and not have them look into my eyes. It was my New York persona, or more aptly stated, my personality shield.

Katherine and I eventually increased our contact, and our conversations were a welcomed distraction. Like the others, Katherine was aware of my marital status and freely chose to continue spending time with me. We didn't engage physically for several weeks. Eventually, Stacy discovered the relationship.

It was a hot Sunday afternoon. It was the kind of hot that challenged the air-conditioner's coldness. I decided that I needed something cold to drink, so I ran out to the local Armenian grocery down the block. Little did I know my thirst would be my undoing. When I returned home, Stacy was visibly angry. She had something in her hand. It was my second phone, my secret second phone. In my haste to quench my thirst, I had forgotten to take it with me. I had left it in my jacket, and the ringer was not turned off. Katherine had called twice and left a follow-up text message asking if I was still coming over to her house tonight. Stacy threw the phone at me. It missed, but it did not break. I could see that Stacy had tried to call Katherine ten times, but after the initial one, lasting only a few seconds, Katherine did not answer any further calls. Katherine must have heard Stacy's voice, realized it was most likely my wife, and not answered any subsequent calls or replied to texts. When I spoke to Katherine the next day, she confirmed that this was in fact what had happened. Stacy demanded that I leave the house and not return. I left home that day.

It felt like my relationship with Stacy was finally over. I did not think it could recover from this. The truth was, I did not want it to end this way, but I did not want it to continue in the manner it was going. I received a call from Katherine the next day. She told me that all this craziness was too much drama for her, and that she would appreciate it greatly if I did not contact her again. In a way I was relieved. I felt that in some sort of demented way, this double breakup was a hidden opportunity for me to start fresh and finally get my act together. Over the next few weeks, I stayed at a series of hotels. I had a lot of time to think about my actions. I had started to believe that I had the intestinal strength to turn the proverbial corner and stay the course of a new me.

During this time, Stacy made a final overture to let me know she was interested in exploring ways to mend our broken relationship. I vividly recall the night. She invited me back home, where she'd cooked a wonderful dinner. She had prepared my favorite dish and was dressed very beautifully. She was not ready to go quietly into that dark night. After dinner we sat on the couch and finally got around to talking about our relationship. Stacy spoke compassionately of healing our broken marriage. She said that both of us had made mistakes, and perhaps in time we could make things right.

It was a painfully difficult moment because even though I still cared about Stacy, I had since decided not to turn back to the marriage. I knew turning back would mean I'd continue living my life as a codependent husband. In fact, the first thing I noticed when I greeted Stacy that night was the faint smell of alcohol on her breath. It took everything in me to suppress my codependent urges to ask her if she was still drinking. I knew if I did that, the dinner would be ruined. I tried to explain to Stacy that even though I still cared for her greatly, turning back to the relationship would not be a healthy decision for either her or me. She did not quarrel or disagree with me. She simply stood silently in front of me for several uncomfortable moments, then kissed me on the cheek and softly told me to have a good life. Her watery eyes ignited my codependent spirit. I probably would have stayed if she had asked me again to do so at that moment. However, she did not. Perhaps deep down, Stacy was ready to finally let go as well. Stacy and I did not speak for at least a year after that night.

I closed my eyes and started walking towards a new and uncertain life.

Three months into that walk, I received a phone call from Katherine. She said she wanted to talk with me. I didn't know what about; perhaps she wanted to start seeing me again. We met at a popular Italian eatery on the Upper West Side. We talked mainly of polite things: the weather, how we both had been since last seeing one another, etc. Oddly, we didn't talk any about the breakup. The only thing she asked concerning my situation was if I was still with my wife. I told her no.

After the restaurant, we went for a walk. We stopped at a park bench on Fifty-Ninth Street and Columbus Circle. She started the conversation lightly, as it had been at the restaurant. Then her manner shifted as she looked me directly in the eyes and told me she was pregnant. Pregnant. I couldn't believe what I was hearing. How could she be pregnant? I blurted out, "You told me . . . assured me that you had that IUD thing inserted after a pregnancy scare many years ago!" I saw a wave of sadness and shame wash across her face. I quickly shifted my tone and manner. I held her hand, asked her what she needed, and said that I wanted to be involved in the child's life.

I'm not sure if I meant that as strongly as I proclaimed. The truth was, I was scared out of my mind. Prior to the knowledge that I'd be a father within seven months, I had been the designated uncle of the family. My sisters' children and even my first cousins' children affectionately called me "Uncle." I enjoyed this title because it afforded me the luxury of being a parental-type figure without the heavy responsibilities of being a "real parent."

Katherine explained that she didn't expect anything from me. She said she told me only because her best friend had encouraged her to do so. Katherine admitted that she was surprised I'd expressed such a strong interest in participating in the child's life. Again, fighting back all my reservations and fears, I strongly claimed this to be the case.

Several months passed, and Katherine and I saw each other more frequently. Our relationship remained platonic during this time. We went shopping for the child, and there was a baby shower hosted by her two closest friends, whom she had known since her college sorority days. It was an awkward event. There I was standing in the middle of her friend's living room celebrating the coming of a child born out of wedlock. For the most part, my child's mother seemed unmoved by this fact, but at different times during the shower, I could see looks of disapproval flash across her various friends' faces.

After the shower, we started double-dating more with her various friends and their significant others. Even though Katherine and I were still "just friends" expecting a child, I was starting to feel like the dynamic was getting ahead of me. Were we a couple now? Part of me knew the answer was no, but the codependent side of me quelled that voice and allowed the relationship to take on a different meaning. I convinced myself this was the right thing to do. A child needed to see both of his or her parents together and living under one roof. Therefore, one week before our baby was born, Katherine moved into my apartment. We were officially a couple. We never declared this to be the case. We simply moved all her belongings into my space. We were a couple, and soon we'd be parents. The expecting mother was equally excited about both realities. Me, I was happy I was finally doing the "right thing."

CHAPTER THREE

A NEW REALITY

The birth occurred without incident. I called my older sister in tears, confessing I wasn't sure if I was ready for this. She reminded me in her no-nonsense but caring manner that I had to get ready because "This is happening." Her advice, short but poignant, helped me to face my new reality, reminded me that I was a father and that I needed to embrace what this change meant. I was scared, but I did my best to hide it. I was grateful my mother had flown out to help me. Here I was becoming a father, and I still needed my mother to help me to maintain balance. Watching the birth of a child is a remarkable experience. I was there and offered whatever small support I could. After hours of labor, our child made her appearance. Our daughter was born November 20, 2009, and she was beautiful. When I held her in my arms for the first time, I thought of the Stevie Wonder song "Isn't She Lovely." I became more than an uncle; I was a daddy.

I cried again. My mother says I get my crying from my paternal grandfather. He'd cry every time he dropped me and my sister back at our mother's home after a long Sunday visit. Now it was my turn. I was the dad. I kissed Katherine on the forehead, told her the baby was beautiful, made sure she was okay, and then made certain all was okay with our child. I followed the doctor into another room, where they would perform follow-up tests on our baby before taking her back to Katherine. I stayed with my daughter, making certain she was well cared for before returning to Katherine's room.

When I returned to the room, I discovered that Katherine had been moved into a semiprivate room. I was escorted to the room by a kind freckle-faced nurse. When I arrived at the room, I saw Katherine holding papers in her hand. It was time to name the baby and record the parents' information. We'd decided on the first name, Kisha, but when I asked the mother what she was planning to record as the child's last name, she said it would be her last name. A surge of shame grew inside of me. Here I was about to be a father, and the child wouldn't carry my last name. Maybe it was ego as well, but I didn't pause to examine those feelings. I acted before Katherine could write down her last name.

I told Katherine I thought the baby should bear my last name because I was planning on asking her to marry me. I'd filed and received the paperwork finalizing my divorce several months prior to Kisha's birth, so the path was clear for me to propose and eventually move forward with a marriage. Katherine cried and told me not to say it if I didn't mean it. In that moment, I convinced myself this was what I wanted, ignoring the fear motivating my actions. I asked her to marry me right there in that recovery room. I told her we'd be married within a year, and all would be okay. She held me close, cried, and said she would marry me. I did not give her a ring at that moment. It would be another few months before that happened. We agreed not to let family and friends know until a later date. I believe Katherine agreed to this because she did not want it said that I had asked her to marry her only out of guilt or some other false motivation. Whether this was true or not, we were now engaged. She agreed to record my last name as the child's last name. For the moment, I was convinced I'd done the right thing. I was convinced I was happy.

The days passed, and we were adjusting to parenthood smoothly. Our daughter made it easy. Of course she cried, but not much during the night hours. Kisha often slept peacefully through the night. We agreed that Katherine would not immediately return to work but instead stay home and care for Kisha. I went about trying to properly provide for three people.

This was a huge shift of responsibility for me. Prior to this, I was accustomed to taking care of myself. Even in my previous marriage, I took care of my portion of the bills and Stacy hers. Now the financial responsibility was squarely on my shoulders. It was a jolt of reality, especially since I'd recently left my glamorous job as a sports agent and was striking out on my own with a good friend and business partner at our newly established management and consulting firm. Initially, business was good, but I soon learned that without the weight of a powerful agency or notable client, people didn't return my phone calls with zeal and agree to lunch meetings as quickly.

The months passed, and money and business continued to evaporate. Pressure was mounting around the house. Katherine wanted to look for a job, but my ego viewed that as a failure on my part. I convinced her not to seek employment. I also convinced her I was eventually going to follow through on my promise to marry her really soon.

I was choosing to move deeper into the rabbit hole even though there were growing signs Katherine and I weren't as compatible as we were pretending to be around her friends and mine. We were arguing more about what she defined as "my lack of effort to fully engage as a parent." She felt that I did not spend enough quality time with Kisha or her. I countered with reasons why I disagreed—such as my excessive work schedule. She would call me a weekend dad who lived at home. Perhaps there was truth in that statement. For the most part, my work schedule allowed me to spend quality time with Katherine and the baby only on the weekend. Moreover, I did not spend that much one-on-one time with Kisha. Most of my time with Kisha, even on the weekends, was spent with both mother and daughter. I did not allow myself to feel guilty about that. I assuaged that guilt by convincing myself that in exchange for quality time, my heavy work schedule allowed Katherine to stay at home and properly bond with Kisha and for us to be financially secure. But as I said, the latter part of that statement was starting to change. Business was drying up. Nonetheless, I was home every night. We never missed a meal, and the lights stayed on. I felt the growing need to remind Katherine of this more frequently. Even though I understood her point of view and tried to increase the time I spent interacting with them, I still needed to work. We started to argue more about these matters. Unfortunately, some of these arguments occurred in front our child, a behavior neither of us wanted to make a habit.

My management and consultant firm's business was at an all-time low around this time. I decided for the sake of my family to find a traditional nine-to-five job. It was a necessary but uncomfortable decision. I'd grown used to the unstructured lifestyle afforded me as an agent, but that business was a thing of the past. I got a job working as a managing career counselor at a young adult training center. The social service compensation wasn't nearly as lucrative as my previous job, but it did offer much-needed financial relief, provided health care for Kisha, and eased some of the tension at home. What it didn't do was lead me to look deeper at the eroding emotional path Katherine and I were still on, a broken path we'd soon discover needed much more than extra household money to repair.

We continued to pretend. There were plenty of outside stimuli to distract us from what was happening in our small world. An example was the midterm elections. Barack Obama had recently been elected president, and we both wanted to make certain that he had congressional and senatorial support. We both volunteered. There were several days when all three of us—me, Katherine, and Kisha (Kisha in her stroller)—hit the campaign trail to do our part to help elect individuals we believed would make meaningful changes in our country and our child's future. Those were exciting times!

Shortly after the election season ended, we decided a family trip was in order. We booked three tickets on a Caribbean cruise ship and set sail. It was the best time of our relationship. We didn't argue once. When we were engaged in activities that distracted us from the deficits of our relationship, it made things seem okay, so we allowed ourselves this moment of brief amnesia.

We returned home and the dust settled. We were alone again with our increasingly dysfunctional relationship. We continued arguing emotionally and physically, distancing ourselves from each other. The dysfunction was starting to play out again in front of our daughter, so we decided to try counseling to help repair our relationship.

The first counselor we saw was an older therapist. Katherine was hesitant about her services after the initial intake because she believed the therapist to be old-fashioned in her thinking. I didn't agree with her assessment. To me, the therapist was insightful and offered sound advice. But the therapy relationship didn't last long. In fact, it ended midway through the first session. The therapist challenged and encouraged Katherine to reframe a long-term personal belief about dating and relationships. I cannot remember exactly what the therapist asked Katherine to challenge, but I do distinctly remember her abruptly getting up and walking out of the session. As I started to walk out, the therapist placed her hand on my shoulder and said, "Good luck." At first I thought I detected sarcasm, but I realized she had said it in a sympathetic tone. Nevertheless, we discontinued her services.

The next therapist was younger. We were in our third session with him when our façade crumbled. I'd become increasingly more uncomfortable with the closeness of Katherine's friendships because she constantly shared all our personal business, including both emotional and sexual. I did not mind her having these friendships. I just wanted these issues vetted in therapy, not over drinks with her old sorority buddies. In fact, this was one of the causes of some of our more heated disagreements.

The therapist suggested that the next time Katherine spoke with her friends, she should refrain from discussing relationship issues without first consulting me about how I felt. She didn't agree with that. She said her friends always shared in this manner, and she would not want to let them down by withholding from them. The therapist challenged Katherine to consider whose level of comfort was more important at this juncture, her friends' or her fiancé's. Katherine continued to insist that her friends wouldn't be comfortable with the suggestion and refused to commit to making it happen.

I didn't say this in the session, but Katherine's refusal to consider placing my feelings first in this matter was disheartening. It also made it difficult for me to fully trust that she was willing to put our relationship first. What I now understand, is that her refusal to curtail her sharing with her friends, stimulated the same feelings of distrust I had experienced when I discovered that Stacy was not following through with her prescribed treatment plan after insisting she was in fact doing so. I chose to ignore the connection between the two dynamics. Instead I focused on the increasing level of distrust I was developing in the relationship every time Katherine mentioned one of her friends.

These feelings of distrust were compounded when I later learned that many of these friends did not want her to be with me.

Perhaps I was overthinking all of this. I too had friends who did not think having a child was reason enough to marry someone. They even tried to convince me not to continue the relationship. But the difference was that I chose to distance myself from those friendships. When I informed the therapist I'd done this, Katherine insisted the only reason I had done so was to force her to do the same. Perhaps she was right, to a small degree. My reason for ending some of my friend-ships might have not been all so altruistic. In fact, one or two (not all, of course) of the friendships that I ended were more acquaintances than friends. The truth is, many of my friends did not know of the full scope of my relationship with Katherine. That was true for many of Katherine's friends and family as well. However, Kathrine's refusal to at least try to understand and somewhat accommodate my concerns regarding her modifying conversation about the deeper inner work-ings of our relationship with her close friends, had caused me to drift further into a state of distrust.

The distrust and our inability to resolve other relationship chal-lenges led me towards more unhappiness. I was starting to feel less and less hopeful about the success of our relationship. Katherine appeared to feel the same way. She rarely smiled around the house anymore. I'd told myself that cheating was not an option in this relationship because it could cost me my daughter, and frankly, I did not want to travel down that road again. So, despite the many warning signs before us, we continued to move forward. We met with wedding planners, took mini–family trips, and continued outings with both her and my friends, to whom we presented ourselves as the happily engaged cou-ple. The truth was, I was spiraling downward, and so was Katherine.

Our masquerade was becoming increasingly unhealthy, especially for Kisha.

I recall one evening when we were arguing in the kitchen while Kisha stood close by. She came into the kitchen and tried to get us to stop, but we didn't. Our three-year-old, raised her arms in the air and shook her hands back and forth, a gesture of helplessness. The sight of Kisha walking away in that manner pierced me. I left the kitchen and went to give her a big hug, assuring her that Mommy and Daddy were okay, and we loved her very much. She smiled. Her smile strengthened my resolve to make things right with her mother.

To that end, I started to attend Al-Anon meetings to address my unresolved issues regarding my ex-wife's depression and my failure to properly handle my role in that process. My level of distrust was heightened because of my failed involvement with Stacy's depression journey. I wanted to do things differently with Katherine. Perhaps she wanted the same. This is probably the reason we agreed to see another counselor.

This time we sought counseling from a life coach, not a licensed marriage and family therapist. Sessions with the life coach helped some. The arguments in front of Kisha significantly decreased. We still argued; however, we both resolved to shield Kisha from those moments. I could tell by Kisha's frequently smiling face and overall happy demeanor that she was pleased with the newfound peace between her parents. However, those sessions weren't helping Katherine and me to grow closer or properly address our mounting displeasure with our relationship. We were still in a negative spiral that was growing deeper and wider as the days trudged on.

The increasing financial needs of our household only escalated tensions further. The training center where I'd been working closed.

We were running close to the end of our savings, and I still didn't want Katherine to work. My ego overshadowed my reality, so I acted quickly. I hit the pavement hard and found a new job, one paying more money. The financial crisis was averted, but Katherine and I still weren't happy. We couldn't come to one accord. We continued to argue about most things. The only silver lining was that these disagreements mostly occurred away from Kisha.

One evening while watching television, Katherine looked over at me and said, "You're going to just keep plowing along with this relationship, huh?" The statement was very clear: we weren't happy, and I should "be a man" and leave. I didn't reply. I continued watching television. The truth was I had prepared to keep "plowing along." I didn't want to be the one who broke up the family. I didn't want my daughter to grow up in a broken home as my older sister and I did.

When I was eleven, I moved from Atlanta to live with my father in Washington, DC. My parents had divorced years before. My mother spoke to me once of the pain caused by the divorce. She said that she really wanted to make the marriage work, but my father's dreams did not align with her wants. She said that moving back to Atlanta with me and my older sister was very hard, but she determined that she would not stay in a relationship when she was not wanted.

My mother's strength to let go would again be tested with me years later. When I was ten, my father began making requests for me to live with him in DC with my older sister continuing to live with our mother in Atlanta. For a while my mother rejected the idea. Then one summer, after the conclusion of a routine summer visit, my father had convinced me that I needed to live with him in DC. So when I went back to Atlanta, I started acting out, skipping school, disobeying my mother, and getting into fights. This went on for several months until one day my mother and father came together to discuss the matter. The result was that my mother agreed to let me move to DC.

Because of this move, I would see my mother and older sister only during holidays and summer vacations. I always immensely enjoyed the times with them. To make certain that I still had quality time with my sister, she would spend only one month with my father during the summer and the other two months would return to Atlanta while I was still there. We spent all holidays in Atlanta. To ensure quality time with my older sister, my father would fly down to Atlanta during some holidays and see her while I was there. My older sister and I remained close by talking on the phone most days and writing each other frequently during the school year.

The visits back to Atlanta were always great. However, seeing the pained expressions on my mother's and sister's faces every time I left Atlanta to return to DC still haunts my thoughts and fills me with guilt. I've since learned that I wasn't the cause of their pain. Yes, seeing me go was painful, but I was not responsible for the dynamic that caused the split in my parents' marriage and their subsequent decision to let me move to DC to live with my father. However, those early feelings of guilt directly affected decisions I'd make in future romantic relationships—specifically with my ex-wife and my child's mother. I was afraid to risk my daughter experiencing this guilt or me not having the opportunity to see her every day.

Like many other men, I dreaded the thought of going to court to pursue child custody because of the horror stories I'd heard. I also had personally witnessed men going to court and losing all rights to see their children. Most of the best-case scenarios I'd heard involved the father receiving only an unsatisfying court-ordered visitation schedule. I knew two personal examples of men experiencing this type of unbalanced court outcome. My old college buddy Elijah received only three days a week with no overnights and very few holidays, and my uncle got only summers. Both these men had been accustomed to seeing their children every day before the court decrees.

I shared their stories with Katherine on one occasion. I'm not certain why. Perhaps subconsciously I was sending a message to her that I didn't want us to go down that path. Sharing their stories turned out to be a mistake. Katherine admonished me to remember the terrible court experiences of Elijah and my uncle on two or three different occasions after I had floated the idea of leaving the relationship and having us work out an equitable custody plan. I didn't mention court, but she'd seize upon the opportunity to remind me of the possibility of sharing my uncle's and Elijah's fates. These "reminders" contradicted her statement about my "plowing along." It reinforced that she was as prepared as I was to remain in this rising dysfunction.

Katherine's admonishment and other urban tales about men getting crushed in family court vanquished the thought of my filing for joint custody or even a fair visitation schedule. I was petrified of the court system. The fact that so many African American men and women had been denied legal parity in the court system throughout America's history only heightened my negative feelings about the justice system. I didn't want to play those odds. I concluded I had a better chance of keeping my daughter connected to me and the experience of a whole family by remaining in this unhappy union.

So I stayed—we both did. I trained myself to suppress my feelings and feigned happiness, especially around our daughter and our friends and family. We didn't let them know how unhappy we were. Katherine did, however, continue to share with a few of her close friends. I continued to voice my objection about that. I was too embarrassed to let anyone know that I was not in control of my affairs. I became isolated from my support system.

I didn't realize we were unconsciously teaching our daughter that even if she was unhappy, she should stick it out. Some would argue a child our daughter's age (at the time she was around three) couldn't understand this concept. I'd counter by saying children are more perceptive than we give them credit for. For instance, our daughter would bring her mother water when she felt Katherine was sad or angry. I noticed she was bringing her mother more and more water. She'd rub my forehead when she perceived I was tired or sad. She didn't see us argue much anymore, but despite my efforts to feign happiness, she sensed that her parents weren't happy. We were like many parents and couples who keep their children trapped in toxic relationship dynamics. As they grow older, they recreate these negative dynamics or seek out individuals with similar negative relationship beliefs. Often the children who are prisoners of unhappy and abusive relationships don't realize they are recreating the dynamics they witnessed until it's too late.

I'd convinced myself my self-worth as a man and father was inextricably tied to staying with my child's mother. With the help of the mother's constant critique of my performance in the home, I mistakenly believed I wouldn't be a good man or a good father if I left the relationship. I didn't allow myself to see the many examples of men who had left their dysfunctional relationships and remained strongly involved in their children's lives. I thought leaving the relationship would create a formidable barrier between my child and me. The idea of going to court didn't help to assuage those negative feelings. I mistakenly believed, and my child's mother often reminded me, that being a good man meant staying with and taking care of not only my child but her as well, something her father had done up until her late teens.

She often spoke of her father in glowing terms during that time of her life, but when he finally left home, she often would say that he had "abandoned the family." I'd adopted Katherine's narrow definition of a good man and good father. Being happy was no longer important to me. Achieving Katherine's definition of a "good man" to secure a relationship with my child was all that mattered.

It would be another two years before I found the courage to leave the relationship, and it was not a simple task.

CHAPTER FOUR

AWAKENING

In pursuit of making a better family life, I accepted a position working as a program developer and community resource partner with a nonprofit organization serving children and families. The pay was greater than my previous job. I cherished being able to provide financially for my family more sufficiently. This position allowed me to continue working with youth and their families, which gave me purpose beyond my role as a father.

Working with youth and families was purposeful, but it was also challenging. I was drawn to helping people solve their problems even though I couldn't get my personal affairs in order. I turned out to be effective and strategic in my approach with helping the families I served. I treated them like individuals. I didn't try to force them to accept a scripted slate of solutions designed to save "poor" families from their tragic plight. In fact, prior to each family coming to our organization, we'd receive a file on the family history. Our three main referral sources were the Office of Children and Family Services (OCFS), probation, and dependency court. I started the practice of not reading the entire family profile. I read the more salient aspects of the file, such as features of the family's history and some reasons why the youth and family required our services. Reading only a portion of the file allowed me to learn about the family's history and current circumstances from them directly. This practice helped to inform the youth and family early in our relationship that I respected and encouraged their right to define who they were and what they hoped to accomplish during our interaction.

As the program developer, I was responsible for organizing the weekly team and family meetings. During these meetings, we—the professional team and the family—strategized options to help the family and youth continue living together safely. The professional team consisted of the program developer, the child specialist (the voice and primary advocate for the youth), the parent partner (the primary support for the parent or foster parent), and a psychologist. This is how I came to know Anyanwu. She was the team's psychologist. She was named after a character from one of Octavia E. Butler's brilliant novels, *Wild Seed*.

I was going into my second year at the organization when Anyanwu came aboard as a psychologist. I'd noticed her around the office. I thought she was attractive. Her warm smile and inviting disposition made her stand out. I didn't speak much with her at first. She later shared that she thought I was indifferent to her by the way I had first greeted her. The truth is she intrigued me, but I wanted to give little or no indication of that because I was trying to be a faithful fiancé to Katherine and do nothing to interfere with keeping my pretend happy family intact. I know that last part sounds harsh, but in truth that's what we were doing—maintaining a charade we'd both learned to represent as real, perhaps for the sake of Kisha's happiness.

I'd learned to be a man of few words. This discouraged people from feeling invited to learn more about my personal life. I disclosed the bare minimum about my home life. The office knew I was a father and had a fiancée, but that was all I'd disclosed. The rest of my office conversation centered on the youth and families we jointly served. However, there was something different about Anyanwu. I was compelled to speak with her, and I couldn't explain why. Perhaps it was the way she challenged me. Once after a review of one of our cases, Anyanwu joked that even though everyone lavished praise on my assessment of the family's dynamics and the plan for the strategies we were employing, I hadn't said anything of substance. She called it "glitter in their eyes." She referenced the performance of Richard Gere from the movie *Chicago* when he sang and danced about convincing a jury of his client's innocence by speaking fancy words but nothing of substance. I couldn't disagree with her. Perhaps it was a throwback to my days as a sports agent. I did care about the youth and families I worked with, but I wasn't a fan of creating lengthy documentation to explain my work with them, so I used my "flashy words" to substitute for some of my absent paperwork.

Anyanwu and I spoke more frequently about our cases. One day I did something surprising; I allowed myself to talk about some of my personal matters. We were at the office, and I asked Anyanwu to join me in the conference room. I disclosed to her the difficulties I was having with Katherine. I didn't go into too much detail; I was still trying to maintain my guarded persona. I asked her if she could recommend a good couples counselor. In truth, I really don't think I'd have followed through on her recommendation. I wanted to be open with someone, and for some reason I chose her. She'd later share how strange this moment seemed. Here I was asking Anyanwu for counselor recommendations to save my relationship with Katherine after months of virtual silence, and she didn't flinch. She listened to me without judgmental looks or patronizing comments. She listened, and I spoke. It was cathartic, and it opened a door I thought I'd shut years before. I felt I could be myself around Anyanwu with no sunglasses, no lies, and no glitter. That was refreshing.

Back at home, Katherine and I continued spiraling further into our dysfunctional rabbit hole, and we were taking our child down on the ride. Despite this reality, I foolishly clung to my decision to stay in the relationship. I allowed myself to keep thinking being a good father meant staying with the mother no matter what, but my ongoing conversations with Anyanwu were making me reassess whether remaining in the relationship was truly healthy. Anyanwu had such a calming presence, it made me, the guarded one, want to talk about more than our shared cases; I wanted to talk about my world, my reality. I was starting to trust her more and more.

At first I didn't talk about my personal life. I'd let a morsel of personal stuff slip in every so often to test Anyanwu's reaction. I didn't want her to think I was getting too personal too quickly; I didn't want to scare her away. I tend to be very intense emotionally. My zodiac sign says that I can be very complicated. Truth is, Anyanwu made me rethink my relationship. It wasn't because I was thinking about escaping from my relationship to be with her. She was married, and I was engaged. I was in the firm mindset of respecting both of our relationships despite the many relational challenges I was experiencing. But our conversations made me realize how healing a quarrel-free conversation could be. She made me laugh, and I missed laughing.

We maintained this work and platonic interaction for months until one day I went to see Anyanwu perform. When I had first met her, a mutual coworker introduced her to me as a TV star. I wasn't familiar with her work, but apparently scores of YouTubers and cable TV fans were. They knew her as an amazing spoken word artist. I wasn't sure what to expect when I arrived at the venue. Anyanwu had graciously invited me and my fiancée to her performance, but Katherine couldn't attend because there was no sitter for our daughter. I wasn't the biggest spoken word enthusiast, but Anyanwu had invited me to a couple of other functions (her thirtieth birthday and another event), and I was unable to attend. She had invited several people from the office on these occasions, so I didn't think she'd notice my absence. Still, I didn't want to miss this performance.

Anyanwu's set came near the end of the evening. I was impressed by the audience's reception of her when she walked onto the stage. She was a crowd favorite. The audience quieted and Anyanwu began. I was immediately struck by her voice. There was power behind every word, and I felt the poem she recited that night was written especially for us. It wasn't, but still, I couldn't move. I was frozen in place watching this amazing woman release spellbinding words from her beautiful mouth. All I could do was watch and cry. I knew at that moment I'd fallen in love with her.

After the performance, Anyanwu and I went to a nearby restaurant to chat before going our separate ways. I knew this conversation would be different. Truthfully, I had almost chosen to avoid this moment, but I didn't. We sat across from each other, awkwardly searching for words to say that would prolong what we were both feeling. I wasn't sure if Anyanwu felt the way I did. Our previous conversations hadn't been flirtatious. We hadn't crossed any inappropriate lines. She respected my relationship and I hers, but that night it was more difficult. I expressed to her what I had felt during her performance and that these feelings were harder to ignore. She expressed to me that she'd fallen for me as well. She said she realized this after the second time I didn't show up at one of the earlier events she had invited me to. She said she felt very disappointed. At first she couldn't explain why, but she finally accepted it was because she had developed strong feelings for me. She was falling in love with me, as I was with her.

After mutually expressing our feelings, Anyanwu paused and said, in the most warm and beautiful way, "So we're in love." I shyly replied yes. We were in love, but we knew we couldn't act on this love. Anyanwu had recently separated from her husband, and I was still living with Katherine, even though by that time we'd decided to quietly end the engagement. So Anyanwu and I were in love with no foreseeable outlet to act on our feelings.

We decided the best thing to do was continue our platonic relationship. We knew this would be difficult, but it was the right thing to do. We spoke for a short while longer, shook hands, and parted ways. I went home and kissed my daughter good night and said our nightly prayers. Kisha was a bit of a night owl, so she was still up playing. I closed her bedroom door, went into the living room, and fell to sleep on the couch. Even though Katherine and I had ceased having intimate relations, we'd still sleep in the same bed to not let Kisha think we were mad at each other. That night, I felt sharing a bed with Katherine would further complicate the already complicated moments Anyanwu and I had just shared. I lay up most of the night thinking about Anyanwu's soft-spoken proclamation that we were in love.

The next day at work was surreal. There I was in the same office seeing the same coworkers, yet all was different. When I saw Anyanwu, it was as if I were in a dream. She was the woman I had seen yesterday in the same cubicle not too far from mine, yet we were different. We had the awesome task of making sure we kept our feelings tucked away so no one in the office would know what was happening between us, and more importantly ensuring nothing happened between us for the sake of everyone involved, especially our respective children.

We decided to get lunch and talk about a plan. The plan we came up with was perfect in theory but flawed in practice. We wouldn't speak about these feelings and see each other only as it related to work. No more after-work conversations and no more lunches. We would truly be coworkers only. We agreed to do this for six months and check in with our feelings after that time. We shook hands and went back to the office.

The next day, at lunch, we accepted the reality that we needed a new plan.

Difficult as it would be, the new plan was the old plan. We'd continue going to lunch and still talk on the phone after work. However, we'd do this with the understanding that we couldn't act on our feelings. We again shook hands and agreed to stay the friendship course. This was the smart move.

Some would argue that I was emotionally cheating. At the time, I would have vehemently denied that. Today I admit we were broadening the margins of platonic friendship, but I didn't allow myself to entertain that thought because it might have caused me to move away from my friendship with Anyanwu, a friendship that was refreshing and healing. There was one expression of feelings we did permit. We'd send each other songs each day via email and text. We called them SOTD (songs of the day). These songs were inspiring and at times expressive of feelings we couldn't act on. This was our way of saying how we felt about each other without saying the words directly. They were our musical Hallmark cards. The first two songs I sent to Anyanwu were "Maria," the song from the classic musical *West Side Story*, performed by Marvin Gaye, and "Time in a Bottle," Jim Croce's timeless hit song.

Another reason we needed this friendship was that we gave each other the space to express difficult feelings without feeling judged or ashamed. These feelings were not solely centered on our personal relationship. Often, because we worked with such a challenging population, our conversations helped us to process many work-related emotions in a healthy manner. When we did process mutual feelings related to our respective relationships, we could allow each other space to express vulnerability, exhaustion, and angst without getting lost in or further emotionally scarred by these emotions. As mentioned, it was cathartic—healing. I believe Anyanwu felt the same.

Meanwhile, matters at home were reaching a critical stage. Katherine and I were no longer talking beyond what needed to be said to maintain household functionality. Sexual relations were a thing of the past. My inordinate distrust continued to fester, mostly due to my own unchecked and unresolved insecurities. She refused to be transparent about outside friendships and her constant berating of my lack of "proper parenting skills." I now understand that the berating was her manipulative way of making me feel inadequate so that I'd be too scared to attempt being a single dad. For a long while, I internalized and believed her version of me as a parent, and it made me feel lousy and inadequate.

Through all this dysfunction, we continued making appearances at many outside events: a Halloween party there, a friend's thirty-fifth birthday party here, the occasional family trip to a local pumpkin patch celebration, or a visit to a local museum. The only silver lining during these times was that Kisha could collect some pleasant memories of her mom and dad together. I'd have felt worse if all the memories of her parents were laced with negative imagery. Despite all the extra padding of social events and trips, we were quickly moving to the realization that our relationship was unsustainable. There was only so much healing a Sunday visit to the park could provide to a badly scarred relationship.

The end was near. I didn't want to face this reality because it meant facing the fact I'd have to try to maintain a relationship with my daughter through her mother. What would that look like? Court directives? Failed parenting experiences? After all, I was "an irresponsible father" according to Katherine. Perhaps we could work out an amicable visitation schedule outside of court. Maybe she wouldn't like the court path either.

I didn't want to find out, but like it or not, the time was quickly approaching. For now, I kept my head low and feelings submerged. I fake-smiled through the uncomfortable moments and continued listening to the occasional Anyanwu SOTD to help make it all seem okay.

CHAPTER FIVE

THE BREAKUP

There's an adage that says, "Whatever is done in the dark will come to light." This is a true statement. At least it was for me one fateful evening.

I received a card from Anyanwu earlier that day. She'd written me a poem. I had left the card in my jacket. Katherine was moving my jacket from the couch, and the card fell out. Katherine stormed into the bedroom, where I was relaxing, and calmly but sternly—asked me what was going on. I immediately froze when I saw the card in her hand. I told her that Anyanwu and I were friends, and nothing physical had ever happened between us, which was the truth. Katherine seemed less concerned about that possibility. She wanted to know if I had fallen in love with Anyanwu. I hesitated for a moment. I knew the next words I uttered could mean a huge life change, a change that would most likely result in my leaving our home. I said, "Yes, I love her."

As I predicted, Katherine insisted that I leave the home immediately. She told me she didn't want to see me any longer, and I'd never see Kisha again. Even though I know these were words many people proclaimed during moments like this, I knew she'd do her best to make those words a reality. As I walked towards the front door, I turned and looked at my daughter's crying eyes and her mother's angry, hurt face. I was miserable. I knew this moment should have happened much sooner, and I felt like a coward for it happening under these circumstances.

Anyanwu's card shouldn't have been the reason I was leaving. The dysfunctional nature of the relationship and the need to keep my daughter away from it should have been the reason. I should have left for our collective mental and physical well-being. I should have had the courage of heart to say to Katherine that happiness was too important a thing for either of us to sacrifice. I was repeating the same pattern of my failed marriage. This time there was a child involved. I was disappointed with myself. I wanted to believe I'd changed, but at that moment I knew very little had.

As I lay in the hotel room that night, I knew nothing would change if I didn't do some serious self-reflection, but how? I didn't have the mental energy to plot out a workable self-healing plan. My mind was preoccupied with thinking about how I'd see my daughter. Would I have to go to court now? Would I lose the chance at a real connection with my daughter? I lay still that night. I didn't watch TV or listen to any music. I was adrift with thoughts about how different things would have been if I had lied when Katherine had asked me if I loved Anyanwu, or if I'd been mature enough to initiate the breakup prior to being outed by the appearance of the card.

For a moment, I became angry with Anyanwu. I was projecting blame onto her. I wanted to call her and ask her why she had given me that card, but I didn't. I couldn't do it because it wasn't her fault; it was mine. In fact, I'd painted a picture so bleak regarding my relationship, Anyanwu believed it would have been only a matter of days before I'd leave the toxic relationship, just as she had the courage to do months prior. Not for me, mind you. Anyanwu had decided on her happiness and on preventing her from becoming a negative example to her young son. She'd packed her bags and moved into her own space, a space we'd eventually call Happiness. Unfortunately, happiness was nowhere in sight for me that night. There was no daughter, no Anyanwu, no SOTDs with loving messages, and no home. I was alone, anxious, and scared of what the morning would bring. If ever someone wished a night would last forever, I believe my desire was to not see the rising sun.

The next day was a workday, and I couldn't avoid going. I had too many clients and team members depending on me. I gathered my things and headed into the office. I hadn't spoken yet with Anyanwu about the breakup. I only sent her a text telling her that Katherine had seen the card she'd given me, and I'd moved out. What I neglected to add was that even though I'd led Anyanwu to believe that my relationship with Katherine was over and we were sharing living arrangements only until she obtained gainful employment, neither I nor Katherine had officially ended our relationship. The engagement, yes, but not the relationship. We were still going on family trips and occasionally sleeping in the same bed without sex, but nonetheless sleeping together.

When I did see Anyanwu, she was confused by my level of anxiousness around the card. She said even though it had been a messy moment, it was good that all was now in the light and that both Katherine and I could start our individual healing processes and hopefully a healthy co-parenting relationship. Anyanwu's optimism didn't last long. Katherine called her at work, and they spoke for at least an hour. After the conversation, Anyanwu told me she needed to speak with me. I was glad she was willing to talk to me but terrified about what she wanted to say.

We took a car ride. We drove a distance without speaking. When Anyanwu spoke, I sensed the profound hurt and disappointment in her voice. She asked me to clearly define the current nature of my relationship with Katherine. I told her we had officially broken up as of the previous night. Anyanwu said Katherine had told her she and I were still a couple and still sleeping together, and I was lying to them both. Anyanwu also told me she had heard Kisha crying in the background while Katherine was talking. Anyanwu asked her if she needed to take a break and go tend to her daughter. Katherine's response troubled Anyanwu, both as a mother and psychologist. Katherine told Anyanwu the child needed to see how hurt her mother was, and it was good that the child knew the truth. Anyanwu considered that a serious red flag. It indicated to her that Katherine wasn't hesitant to wrap her child into her emotional experience, even if that experience was too advanced for the child to properly process.

Anyanwu asked me if I had ever noticed Katherine doing this before. I recalled a few occasions when this occurred. However, I didn't make a distinction between those actions and the times we'd argue in front of Kisha. At the time, I didn't grasp how this aspect of Katherine's behavior could create a lasting, negative effect on Kisha, just as serious as the arguments. I didn't comprehend the extent of the toxic effects of our relationship because I was too enmeshed in our collective family dysfunction.

Anyanwu returned to talking about us. I told her it was true Katherine and I weren't happy and hadn't been happy for a very long time. Yes, we were still going through the motions of a relationship; however, it was merely a show for our friends and families, and more sadly for Kisha. For Anyanwu, no matter what level of truth I chose to reveal about my relationship, if it was not the entire truth, it was deception. She believed deliberately omitting parts of the story to fit a desired narrative was in fact deception. She was right; I had deceived her. I had to own my truth. I couldn't razzle-dazzle myself out of this moment. I didn't want to. I wanted to place it all on the table. If I was going to start facing my demons, demons I'd been evading so many years, demons that had prevented me from being the most authentic person I could be, I had to tell Anyanwu the entire unadulterated truth.

So I did.

"Yes, we are still in a relationship."

That's how I started. I acknowledged my lie. The fact that the relationship was severely broken didn't mean we weren't actively feeding it. It was extremely difficult for me to look Anyanwu in the eyes as I spoke. Normally, I relished getting lost in her eyes, but this moment was different. I was afraid if I saw her beautiful eyes looking at me with disappointment, or worse disgust, I'd revert to razzle-dazzle mode and start lying. So I kept my gaze ashamedly low and told Anyanwu I'd been afraid to leave the relationship because I didn't want to face the possibility of losing my daughter. I told her that I did at one time care for Katherine. I explained to her that the time I'd spent with Katherine in the beginning of our relationship had allowed me to be with someone I could talk to without thinking about needing to save or heal her. Anyanwu knew the history of my marriage and could appreciate my need to want a normal relationship dynamic. However, she wouldn't allow me to use this as an escape route to get out of the conversation or as a valid reason to practice deception.

I explained that shortly after Kisha was born, I started to realize my relationship with Katherine was not healthy. I told Anyanwu that Katherine and I had tried to repair our relationship, but we'd finally settled on emotional mediocrity. Even though this meant continued unhappiness for us both, I was prepared to make unhappiness work if it meant keeping my daughter in my life and out of court.

I explained to Anyanwu that I wasn't prepared for her. I told her she made me want to live in my truth, and I was trying hard to do that. I clarified to Anyanwu that in my not-so-distant past, I wouldn't have tried to prevent a romantic relationship with her. I would have crossed that proverbial line a long while back, perhaps during the night I first saw her on stage. I told her the reason I didn't was that I felt if I stayed the course, I could keep what was happening between us "pure," and if the chance did arise for us to be together, we'd have a different type of relationship from the ones we'd experienced. Keeping my relationship with Anyanwu "pure" and keeping Kisha in my life ironically made me do the very thing I'd been working to change. I was being dishonest with Anyanwu and Katherine, and Katherine and I were being dishonest with each other and our friends and families. Moreover, I was being dishonest with myself.

I told Anyanwu I'd made progress. I knew being in a toxic relationship was unhealthy for my daughter, but I was scared to face the potential consequences of losing her. So I misrepresented the nature of my relationship with Katherine to Anyanwu and others. After a while, it became easier to lie. I justified this by convincing myself that the absence of physical contact in my interactions with Anyanwu and Katherine meant I wasn't cheating on either of them. Convoluted thinking, I know. But I wanted to keep Anyanwu and my child in my life while feeling like I was a good guy.

I told Anyanwu I wanted this deception to end. I wanted to work towards being the good guy that I had pretended to be. I'd made a habit of misdirecting people away from my faults. It was an exhausting way of life. This lifestyle prevented me from working to improve on these faults, allowing them to sprout like wild weeds and stifle my growth. I wanted to be a better self-gardener, and I told Anyanwu having her in my life was healthy motivation in that direction.

She was quiet. Her silence felt like it would go on forever. I mustered the courage to look up at her. She was staring directly at me. I didn't know what to say. Anyanwu must have noticed my agony and granted me mercy. She finally spoke. She said as a psychologist, she understood the motivations behind my actions, but she couldn't condone or excuse my actions. She said I had hurt her, and I could see the pain in her eyes. She said she needed some time to process all of this and asked me to give her the time without interference. We knew we had to continue working together, so some contact couldn't be avoided. But all other contact needed to cease until she was ready to engage me, if that time ever came again. This meant no more lunches, no more after-work conversations, no more SOTDs . . . no more Anyanwu, at least for now.

A couple of days after the initial breakup incident, Katherine contacted me via text to let me know Kisha wanted to see me. I had texted her earlier and let her know I was sorry about what had happened, and I wanted to see Kisha as well. I tried calling, but Katherine wouldn't take my call. Via text, we planned for me to see Kisha the next day.

I was still staying at the hotel. When I arrived to pick Kisha up, Katherine and I exchanged only a few words. She asked me what had happened between Anyanwu and me, and I told her our friendship appeared to be over. She asked me if I still thought I was in love with Anyanwu, but I didn't want to answer out of fear of her becoming upset again and demanding I leave before I had the chance to see our daughter. Thankfully, she didn't press the issue. Perhaps she could see the answer in my eyes. Either way, the moment was uncomfortable for us both. Seeing my baby girl run excitedly towards me made all the wrong in my life seem right. She jumped into my arms, screaming, "Daddy, Daddy!" We drove around and hung out for a few wonderful hours.

Eventually, Katherine and I decided on an unofficial, non-court-ordered visitation schedule. I'd see my daughter three times a week for three hours on Monday, Wednesday, and Friday. I'd pick her up from day care around 5:00 p.m. and drop her off at home at 8:00 p.m. The schedule was difficult. I had to travel over forty to fifty miles each of these days to make it work, but I didn't complain to Katherine. I wanted to see Kisha, and this was the way it had to happen for now.

Most of our time together during these brief visits was spent in parks, restaurants, museums, and libraries. It was a totally different experience. Prior to this, I had seen my daughter every day. At home, we would play make-believe games, build castles, and watch her favorite TV shows like *Barney* and *Yo Gabba Gabba!* She was accustomed to seeing me, her dad, every day and I her. I remember one night when we were having dinner, Kisha simply would not eat her food. Katherine and I both tried the baby talk method of persuasion, by eating the food from her plate to make her know it was good. Still she did not eat. So I put on my best Barney the purple dinosaur voice and told her I was there to help her eat all her dinner. First it did not work. However, after a few moments, she began to laugh and eat. We spent the better part of thirty minutes doing that, but it was worth it. She finished her dinner. Those were the moments I truly missed. I did not feel like a whole father parenting on budgeted time outside of our home.

Having a parental experience on a limited time schedule and via restaurants and parks was indeed extremely challenging, but somehow, we made it work. Something funny happened during this time. I noticed other dads and their children at some of the locations my daughter and I would visit. At first, I didn't pay too much attention to the other dads and their children. Eventually I could tell if the dads were on a visit as I was. Maybe it was the partially stressful look that these dads wore on their faces. Perhaps it was a dad helping his child out with his or her homework or the hurried way some of the dads gathered the children at the end of the visit. On a couple of occasions, I asked a few of the dads if they were on visits with their children, and most confirmed they were. I said I was as well. It felt strange. I didn't know these gentlemen. They were of all ages and races. But once we knew that we were in the same situation, we were connected. The connection was simply an understanding that we were doing what had to be done to stay connected and bonded to our children.

Seeing these other dads from time to time made me feel less isolated even though much of my isolation was self-imposed. It was difficult to talk to family and friends about my situation. I was embarrassed and frankly didn't want to impose my misery on them. It made me realize that for me to get through this new phase in my parenting experience, I needed support—perhaps some type a fatherhood group. Little did I know that I was about to discover how much support I truly needed.

CHAPTER SIX

ALLEGATIONS

For a time, the visits went without incident. I'd pick up Kisha from preschool and drop her back off at Katherine's home at the agreed-upon time. It became our new normal. I even regained some level of pleasant verbal exchanges with Katherine during the drop-offs. We wouldn't speak long; short talks were less uncomfortable. I attended dinner on a few occasions with Kisha and Katherine at their home. I knew dinner wasn't the best idea, but I figured if we were on a peaceful path, why rock the boat? Again I rationalized it would be good for our daughter to see her mother and father getting along. This changed about a year after our breakup.

Around this time, Anyanwu and I began taking small steps towards reconnecting with each other on a personal level. We still worked at the same agency, but Anyanwu had transferred to a different office location shortly after she learned the truth about my relationship status with Katherine. Anyanwu and I would talk from time to time, but it was strictly work related. I'd see her during agency-wide meetings and for biweekly team consultation, but we shared only one case together now.

I found myself missing her more and more. She made difficult conversations easy, and she was invigorating to be around. Her smile made me want to be a better person. I wanted that feeling back in my life. I wanted Anyanwu back in my life. Therefore, I gathered all the courage I could and asked her to attend a lecture at a local college with me, a lecture featuring my father. My father had moved to New York a few years before me. He had secured a teaching position at City College of New York. He taught acting there and was giving a lecture on the history of Black people in theatre. Surprisingly and thankfully, Anyanwu agreed.

Being with Anyanwu outside of the office was a delight. I admit, it was scary as well. I battled butterflies in my stomach the entire time. I wanted to say and do all the right things so she'd see I'd made emotional progress since we had last connected on this level. The night was perfect; she was perfect. She and my father even enjoyed a great conversation after the lecture.

Days after the lecture, Anyanwu and I connected more on the phone and eventually started meeting each other for lunch. It was different from before, and we both knew that. We couldn't erase the past. It was there as a lesson for us both. For me the lesson was to live in truth. For Anyanwu it was to be true to her instincts. Anyanwu shared that she suspected something was incomplete about how I had described my relationship with Katherine, but she had allowed her feelings for me to overshadow her instincts. She said the time spent apart from me had helped her to own this. We also had to admit the feelings we'd had prior to the incident were still there. As Anyanwu had so sweetly declared at that Denny's restaurant after her performance, we were still in love. The question was what to do with this love. Anyanwu was no longer married, I was one year separated from Katherine, and we were both parents. We agreed we wouldn't reveal our relationship to anyone, not even our friends or family. We'd see how things developed before "going public," if that ever happened. This was a way to truly connect with each other minus the pressure of outside forces, even our well-meaning friends and loving family members.

This plan worked for a while. We were embroiled in an amazing period of emotional and spiritual exploration. We met for lunch daily, and every Thursday I'd go to Anyanwu's house, where we'd watch movies, eat dinner, stay up late talking, and enjoy being happy. In fact, we started calling her home Happiness. It was a good time. Visits with Kisha were going smoothly, but the closer I got to Anyanwu, the more I decreased extra contact with Katherine. I eventually ceased all dinners with her, hoping to avoid any confusion about my intentions. I continued my visits with Kisha, but not at Katherine's home. Even though Katherine didn't verbally say it, I sensed she had started to feel comfortable with having me in the home again.

I was correct. Katherine made a startling proposal one time when I dropped Kisha off. She suggested that we take another family trip, this time to the Grand Canyon. She said the trip didn't mean we were back together; it would be two friends who happened to share a child taking a trip. She said it would be a good experience for our daughter. I was confused. My initial reaction was to scream no, but I didn't. I reluctantly agreed that a trip to the Grand Canyon could be good for our daughter. My mind had slipped back into its previous mindset: *If I go on this trip, it will keep the peace, and it will let her know I'm willing to be a team player, a good co-parent.*

The truth is one doesn't have to compromise good boundaries or diminish one's truth to be a good anything, especially a good parent or co-parent. My next thought was, *How will I explain this crazy-ass plan to Anyanwu?* I told Katherine I'd think about it.

The next day, I spoke to Anyanwu about the Grand Canyon plan. As suspected, she didn't view it as a healthy idea. As a psychologist, she

49

said that two separated parents blurring lines this way could create a false narrative for the child, which would eventually lead to the child experiencing more confusion and possibly increased resentment once the truth was revealed. That was her therapeutic response. On the flip side, as my budding girlfriend, she emphatically shut the idea down. She said that she was surprised I'd even consider such a plan. I tried to explain my thinking, but Anyanwu quietly shook her head in disagreement. She let me talk through my entire crazy line of reasoning and asked one question: *"Are you considering this trip and having all those dinners because you're afraid to go to court and secure your rights as a father?"*

Anyanwu's candor frustrated me. Her intention was to make me feel uncomfortable about circling that dangerous rabbit hole again. I told her I needed a moment to think about things, and I'd contact her later. She didn't try to stop me, which angered me. I really didn't want to leave. I wanted to stay. I wanted Anyanwu to tell me the Grand Canyon trip was not such a bad plan. I was looking for her permission to continue being complacent. I was asking her to deny a part of herself that I was deeply in love with: her commitment to the truth. She was right to let me leave.

Still, the truth of her question hit me like a ton of bricks. Was I afraid to go to court? Hell yes, I was afraid to go to court! Statistically the odds weren't in my favor. Custody proceedings typically favored the mother. This was changing some, especially in states such as California but not so much in New York yet. I wasn't prepared to play the odds. I wasn't ready to risk losing additional time with my daughter or having Katherine in complete legal control of our child. Even though she was in de facto complete control at this time, I wasn't ready to admit it.

I took the coward's route, and I went to the Grand Canyon. I told Anyanwu I needed space (three cowardly days to be exact) to figure out some things and work through this moment. Anyanwu didn't challenge me. I wish she would have because I wasn't being honest. I was taking space so I wouldn't feel as if I were cheating on her when I went to the Grand Canyon. I was so afraid of going to family court, I was propelling myself back into the rabbit hole while putting my relationship with Anyanwu back in jeopardy. It was not one of my brightest moments. I went to the Grand Canyon for the weekend, and each moment I thought about how shameful I felt for being there under such circumstances.

Katherine and I argued the entire trip. The spirit and energy were nothing like the boat trip. It was a disaster, and on top of that, I had lied to Anyanwu to make it happen. A few days after the trip, I told Katherine we couldn't do things like family trips anymore. I told her we needed to keep lines clear so Kisha didn't get confused about what was happening. Katherine said I was saying that only because I must have had someone in my life. She asked if it was Anyanwu. I told her no. I was trying to live in truth, so I momentarily convinced myself the space I'd asked Anyanwu for, meant we weren't together; therefore, I wasn't "lying," or so I told myself.

When I returned from the Grand Canyon, riddled with indignity, I reached out to Anyanwu and asked for another chance. I told her that taking space was a selfish thing for me to have done. I thanked her for being patient with my ambivalence. She was not a foolish woman. She would never knowingly allow me to engage her disrespectfully or deceitfully. She'd experienced her share of dysfunction in her own family dynamics, so she was incredibly skilled at separating fact from fiction. She could understand where I was coming from but wouldn't enable my behaviors. After returning from the Grand Canyon, I appreciated this aspect of her character even more.

We resumed communication, but I often wondered if Anyanwu knew the real reason for the space. Years later, I did share the truth with her. Remarkably, she forgave me. I think Anyanwu's heightened sense of spirituality allowed her to move passed my past state of sick thinking. Anyanwu always saw the man I could become. But at the time, I was not that man. I was not a courageous soul. I did want to be with Anyanwu, but I did not want an open battle with Katherine. The levels of deception I allowed myself to create to avoid facing conflict and court were tremendous. However, I was growing weary of this behavior. The universe must have known this because a simple phone call changed everything.

My father and Katherine had developed a somewhat friendly and respectful relationship. She reached out to him one night after Grand Canyon to catch up. My father took the call, hoping to do his part to maintain the peace and keep his granddaughter connected to her paternal family. During their phone call, my father told Katherine about his lecture and about meeting my coworker Anyanwu. He innocently shared that she had attended the lecture with me. I received a text from Katherine, I assume immediately following the call, which read, "You took that bitch to your father's lecture." I did not reply. No further text came, so I unwisely thought I had avoided a more serious bullet. I was sorely mistaken.

The next day, I called my father to see if he had in fact told Katherine about the lecture. He confirmed he had. He said he didn't know he wasn't supposed to speak about Anyanwu. He assumed she was just a friend from work—our behavior at the lecture had led him to believe nothing different. I wanted to be angry with my father, but he wasn't responsible for my deception. I hadn't spoken to him about the circumstances of my breakup or about my fears of court. I had hidden these things from my father and other family members and friends. I told my father he hadn't done anything wrong because it was the truth.

Katherine's behavior towards me radically shifted. I immediately felt this change. Three days after that scathing text, Katherine texted me again, saying she didn't want me to go to our daughter's upcoming doctor visit because she didn't feel safe around me. She claimed she wanted to start making the exchanges with Kisha in a public area for safety reasons. No matter how many texts I sent trying to convince her that there was no reason to be afraid of me, she added layers to this fear narrative with every phone call and text interaction. I called Anyanwu to discuss my concerns.

Anyanwu advised me to file for my parental rights. I didn't want to do that. I thought I could convince Katherine that no matter what had occurred between us, we needed to keep working peacefully with each other for Kisha's sake. I tried this line of reasoning, but Katherine was unmoved, and the texts alluding to her fear of me kept coming.

One day at a routine drop-off, Katherine stood several feet from me. She was too far for me to release our daughter to her, so I walked Kisha closer. Katherine walked further away into the street, saying she was afraid of me. Cautiously, I walked Kisha to the door of her apartment building and waited until Katherine came close enough for me to release our daughter to her.

I spoke to Anyanwu about the incident, and Anyanwu told me she strongly believed Katherine was about to file some sort of court action against me, if she hadn't already. I didn't want this to be the case, but instinctively I knew Anyanwu was right. The time had come.

That night I wrestled with my fear of court. I thought about the negative outcomes, including losing custody of Kisha. Legally, mothers do not have to establish their parental rights, but that was not the case for fathers. In New York, if he was not married to the mother at the time of the child's birth, he needed to file in court for the establishment of his parental rights. This was the path I'd have to take to ensure I wouldn't be left with a day or two here and there to see Kisha, or worse, losing the right to see her at all. Eventually my fear subsided, and I fell asleep. I awakened to a text from Katherine informing me that she didn't want me to attend Kisha's dental appointment because she didn't feel safe around me. My decision was made.

As I stood in line at the courthouse, my heart raced with anxiety. This was it. I knew there was no turning back. I'd prepared myself for the experience by contacting my sister, who practiced law in Atlanta. She gave me as much information as she could about the process of filing for parental rights based upon her understanding from the state where she practiced. The main thing she told me was that I was doing the right thing, and she was there for me. Like her advice to me when I had called her right before my daughter was born, her words strengthened me.

The first thing I learned was that before I filed for visitation and legal custody, I needed to file paperwork legally establishing that I was Kisha's father. As I mentioned, even though my name was listed on the birth certificate as the father, the extra paperwork was a required first step if the parents weren't married at the time of the child's birth. Once filed, I'd be able to file requesting my custodial rights. Luckily, the lady at the front window was kind and explained to me that both filings could be done simultaneously. She must have noticed my nervousness. She told me I could file for a fee waiver if needed. I needed, so I did. A partial fee waiver was granted. After the filing, I went up to another room and paid thirty-five dollars to have the sheriff's office serve the paperwork to Katherine. The filing was done. The next step was to wait.

I didn't have to wait long. Two weeks after filing, I received a knock on my apartment door at 6:00 a.m. It was a sheriff announcing he was there to serve me with papers. Katherine had filed an emergency restraining order. I was legally forbidden to come near her or Kisha.

I was petrified. I tried to read the details of the order, but my mind couldn't make sense of it. All I understood was I couldn't see my daughter until the court date, which was over thirty days away. I called my sister for quick legal advice. I faxed her the court order. She called me and explained that Katherine was asserting she was a victim of domestic violence, and my behavior at the most recent drop-off and in recent times had endangered her and Kisha's safety.

The wait was over. Anyanwu was right. Katherine's recent talk of fearing me had led to court action. I needed more information, so I took the day off from my job and went to the courthouse where the summons had been drawn. The court agent explained that the temporary restraining order would remain in effect until the court hearing, and I couldn't contact or go near Katherine or the child until the matter was resolved. I asked the court worker how this order had been granted without my having the opportunity to counter any of the allegations. She explained that the judge had granted the order for the child's and mother's safety but had made it temporary pending further evidence. I was overcome with fear and growing hopelessness. I feared that my relationship with my child as I knew it was finished.

As I departed the courthouse with those negative feelings welling up inside me, I knew I could not handle this situation by myself. I needed to secure legal counsel. If I had been back in Atlanta, this would have been a simple task. I would have called my sister and let her handle it. In New York, I didn't know where to start. There are jokes about there being too many lawyers in the world, but when you need one, those jokes aren't funny or true. I knew three or four lawyers from my days in the sports industry and from my current job, but I didn't want to approach them. I didn't want my personal business to become public. I was still struggling with irrational pride. On the one hand, I knew I needed help; on the other hand, I was too prideful to reach out to my immediate network for help. Therefore, I started my lawyer search online.

I researched and met with several attorneys. I needed to identify an attorney who was not only within my budget but who would also be passionate about helping me secure my parental rights. I grew weary of this process very quickly. Most of the attorneys I met with, were interested only in discussing their legal fees. The one or two attorneys displaying some level of concern about my current plight were too expensive for me to secure their services. I knew that if I were going to secure an attorney, I had to swallow my pride and reach out to my network for family attorney referrals.

I sent a discreet email to a couple of friends. I didn't go into much detail. I explained enough so they could point me in the right direction. This search guided me to an attorney named Yolanda. We spoke via phone, and I got a good vibe from her. She was empathetic and knowledgeable, and I could afford her retainer fee. I know there are some who might be saying money shouldn't be a factor in a situation like this, but at the time I had to keep it in mind because I was facing a potentially long, drawn-out court battle, and such a battle could cost several thousands in legal fees. So again, I was thankful her legal fees were reasonable.

When I met face to face with Yolanda and discussed the case at length, I was convinced she was the attorney I needed. She didn't rush me when I was discussing the case. She didn't bring up fees until I asked the question. Lastly, near the end of our consultation, she warmly said, "Don't worry; we'll get your baby back to you." I cried so hard. Hope came back into my heart. It was nearing the third week, and I hadn't heard from or seen Kisha. My thoughts were starting to slip into unhealthy spaces, like what if Katherine had taken her to another state or, God forbid, another country? What if I never heard from my child again? I needed to know I was wrong about this wayward thinking, and Yolanda's words gave me great comfort.

Yolanda went right into action. She drafted a response to the mother's domestic violence petition, filed it, and got one of her private investigators to serve Katherine with the response papers as well as the court papers I'd previously filed in family court. The sheriff's department had made three attempts (their maximum) to serve her those court papers to no avail.

Even though Yolanda drafted the petition, I significantly contributed to its content. Once I had realized Katherine was shifting her behavior towards me, such as stopping me from attending medical appointments and proclaiming that she feared me, I started to save all emails and text messages. I also started writing down times I'd pick up and drop off Kisha for our visits and write down any out-of-sorts comments Katherine would make during these times. I didn't know if I'd ever have to use this collected information, but I wanted to be prepared. Thankfully, my instincts were correct. Yolanda told me my journal notes, texts, and emails helped her better frame her response. Yolanda said that as she reviewed my texts and emails, it occurred to her that all my responses to Katherine's texts and emails were very civil. I shared with Yolanda that even though at times I was filled with anger and hurt, I didn't allow those emotions to override my attempt to remain peaceful with Katherine. I believed then and still do now that in the end, civility is more effective than anger. Yolanda agreed. She said that too often in court, fathers place themselves at a disadvantage by expressing their emotions too angrily. Yolanda said when this happens, a judge often sees an angry, scary man, a person who shouldn't be exposed to a child without protective measures, instead of a caring and loving father. Those words stayed with me.

After the serving and filings, I had to wait for the domestic violence hearing. That date was another three weeks away. It had already been five weeks since I'd seen or heard from Kisha. Even though Yolanda's involvement in the case and Anyanwu's growing support made me feel more hopeful, my heart was still hurting. I missed my Little Monkey Man, my nickname for Kisha—silly name, I know. I had once heard Bart Simpson call Homer that name and thought it was so funny. One day Kisha was swinging in the park during one of our visits, and that name, Little Monkey Man, jumped into my head. She laughed so hard when she heard it, I just kept using it. But now there was no laughter. There was no Little Monkey Man around. Only sadness surrounded my heart.

One night while watching a movie about a father and his daughter at Anyanwu's home, I fell apart. The circumstances in the movie didn't mirror my legal situation, but the closeness of the father and daughter in the film was similar, which sent me to a deeply depressed place. I found myself crying profusely and unable to finish the movie. I had gone from a dutiful father who saw his daughter daily to a father with no contact with his child. Two months earlier, this would have been unimaginable to me. Even on the days I didn't have a visit with Kisha, I called and did nightly prayers with her. Now all I had of my daughter were phone recordings and pictures. The sense of loss was profound. I thought about all the fathers in my position and cried. No father who wants to be a father and proves worthy to be a father should be unjustly prevented from exercising his rights to be in his child's life.

I know I couldn't stay in that sad place; it was too emotionally paralyzing. Anyanwu suggested I find a support group where I'd have a healthy outlet to express these feelings. I searched and found a fatherhood support group close to my home. I didn't know what to expect. I thought I'd hear a few sad stories like mine and perhaps hear one or two fathers express some real emotions about their situations. Men aren't the best at expressing their emotions, so I wasn't expecting a large amount of sharing. I was wrong. My first meeting was cathartic. I heard stories like mine and stories that were even more severe. There were some fathers who hadn't seen their children for years. These fathers weren't afraid to display real emotions. Many were crying as they spoke about their children and the deep hurt they lived with due to not being able to see their children. They spoke about the difficulties of navigating family court and child protective services as men in general and men of color specifically. They spoke about bias against them as they struggled to convince the legal system they could be good influences in their children's lives.

For a moment I was discouraged. But the feeling didn't linger because the conversation moved towards proactive strategies that helped many of the fathers survive and prevail when faced with family court and child protective services. The message echoed was to stay cool and not display anger. Anger sends the message you're a potential threat to your child. Many of the fathers encouraged one another to not give up, even if they suffered defeat after defeat. One father said it took him five years to regain partial custody of his two boys—five years, and his spirit wasn't broken. A sense of warmth came over me. I looked at the resolve plastered on the faces of the fathers around me: Black, White, and Latino, young and old. I knew that even if the road to get my daughter back was long and difficult, I had to stay the course like the valiant fathers around me.

I left bursting with determination and buoyed by the prayers of the fathers in the meeting. My fears and anxiety about the court no longer mattered. What mattered was that my daughter deserved to have a good father in her life, and I wasn't going to let anyone stop me from making that happen. The next morning, I received a call from Yolanda informing me she had gotten the court date moved up to the coming week. The stage was set. It was time to go to court.

CHAPTER SEVEN

DOMESTIC VIOLENCE COURT

"**Y**our Honor, the measure of a good father should be determined by his proven love and devotion to his child, his willingness to make sacrifices for that child, and his tireless efforts to make certain he provides for his child to the best of his abilities. This is the type of father standing before you this morning: not a criminal, not an abusive or neglectful father, but a loving and devoted man who wants to be a father to his child."*

Sitting in the cold court hallway awaiting my attorney's arrival, I recalled saying those words in defense of a father assigned to one of my cases. I had witnessed the look of fear in his eyes as he stood before the judge awaiting her decision on whether he'd be reunited with his child or if he had to wait additional time. Powerlessness stained his face like an unfinished painting. At the time, I couldn't imagine I'd ever be in his position. But here I sat outside the courtroom waiting my turn to face a judge. I prayed for the ability to display the same confidence I'd mustered for my client when my turn came to face the judge and plead for my right to continue being a good father. I felt a familiar sense of crippling fear rising in my mind. I knew the paranoia of thinking about losing my child forever wasn't far behind. Thankfully, my attorney exited the elevator at that moment. Discussing courtroom strategy was the distraction I needed.

As my attorney and I conferred, I happened to look up as Katherine and her attorney were entering the courtroom. She glanced over in my direction, but I wasn't certain if she saw me. If she did, she offered no emotional response. My anger grew. Who gave her the right to take my child away?

"I am a good father, and she knows it," I fumed as heat rushed through my veins. I wanted to run over and demand she stop all this madness. Yolanda sensed my reaction. She told me feeling angry was a natural and understandable emotional response at that moment. However, I needed to resist the urge to act on it. She reminded me that displaying anger in the courtroom would be all the validation the court needed to grant an extended restraining order against me, which could mean months or longer without seeing my daughter. She advised me to take my passion and determination into the courtroom but to leave the anger outside. I closed my eyes for a moment and pictured Kisha's tiny, beautiful face. I took several deep breaths, quietly said the Serenity Prayer I had learned from my Al-Anon meetings, and then turned to Yolanda and told her I was ready.

Even though I'd been in dozens of courtrooms supporting my clients, it was as though this was my first time. I noticed everything: the clock on the wall, the bailiff and court stenographer sitting in their appointed seats, and, of course, the judge's bench. I looked around at the faces of the many attorneys sitting in the front of the courtroom and other anxious people, both petitioners and respondents, filling the other courtroom seats. I noticed the American flag to the right of the judge. Lastly, I noticed the huge round, silver-plated seal behind the judge's large brown seat, which read, "The Great Seal of the State of New York—In God We Trust."

I was raised Baptist, and even though I was not an active churchgoer, I believe in God, which I now refer to as my "higher power." I prayed as the court officer called Katherine and me up to the court

bench. It was our turn. As I approached the court bench, I could liter-
ally feel my legs buckle. I thought I was going to fall or freeze. When
I was instructed to raise my hand to swear I'd tell the truth, my hands
trembled. I hesitated for a moment. I didn't want Katherine or her
attorney to see my hand shaking in such a scared manner. The court
officer repeated his instructions, so I complied.

The judge read the details of the allegations and allowed Katherine's attorney to speak first. Katherine's attorney was very sharply
attired. He looked as if his legal representation cost a lot of money.
He resembled one of those expensively dressed attorneys I'd met with
and couldn't afford. However, when he spoke I didn't hear the level of
bravado and brashness I expected. There was a slight hesitation in his
voice. I was puzzled. He didn't appear to be the type of attorney who'd
walk into a courtroom ill prepared. As he continued to speak, I noticed
Katherine interrupting him in an irritated manner. Each time she interrupted him, the attorney changed the direction of his comments.
He appeared to be uncomfortable with her interactions. The judge's
shuffling her papers rapidly back and forth told me she was perhaps
agitated as well.

When it was time for Yolanda to speak, I kept quiet. I let Yolanda go over the reasons I was asking the court to dismiss the restraining order. I'd watched at least three cases in that courtroom before
I was called. I observed the judge grow increasingly annoyed if one
side would speak out of turn or take too long explaining their points. I
didn't want to rock the boat if the boat didn't need rocking. After both
attorneys concluded their comments, the judge rendered her decision.
Each word she spoke seemed an eternity. She said because the peti-
tioner (me) had already filed in family court, she didn't want to render
a decision on the restraining order because after hearing both sides,

she believed the two cases should be merged. I was confused about whether or not this was a good thing. On the one hand, the restraining order was not ratified or extended, which was good. On the other hand, not getting to see my daughter until the date of that next court hearing was sustained agony.

Yolanda requested that my visits with Kisha resume. The judge said whereas she was inclined to grant that, the family court hearing was only a week away, so she'd let the family court judge decide further on the matter, including visitation schedules. Outside court, I felt partial relief. I quickly asked Yolanda to explain if this decision was favorable or not. At that moment, Katherine's attorney motioned for Yolanda to come over to speak. Katherine had already departed the courtroom floor. After a few moments, Yolanda came back over. She told me the attorney had shared with her that he'd asked Katherine if she wanted to allow me to resume visits while we awaited the family court hearing, and Katherine empathically said no. He also shared with Yolanda that this case seemed like a woman scorned more than a domestic violence matter. Both Yolanda and I were shocked at the attorney's candor. It explained his hesitation and back and forth with Katherine in the courtroom. Yolanda explained the decision was a step in a positive direction, that even though the judge didn't resume my visitation rights, she didn't make the restraining order permanent. Yolanda said this was a good thing. She also said it was a great thing I had filed first. Filing first allowed this judge the option to move the case from domestic court to family court. *I was glad that I hadn't succumbed to the fear telling me not to file.*

After court, I had only a week or so before family court. Yolanda was a very capable attorney. She was thorough in her brief preparation and highly skilled in her verbal delivery. I needed my other attorney with me, though, the attorney I had known all my life: my big sister. She couldn't stand up in court as my legal defense, but she had always been there throughout my life whenever I faced seemingly insurmountable challenges. She was there when I was nine and being bullied at school; she was there when we lost our younger first cousin and grandfather; she was there as a protector, a friend, and a shoulder to cry on. I needed her now. True to her protective big-sister nature, when I made the call, she jumped on a plane and was in New York within three days.

Our father picked my sister up from the airport, and we met at my attorney's office, where we were scheduled to discuss legal strategy for the upcoming family court hearing. Seeing my big sister filled me with relief and joy. I held her tightly and thanked her for coming. She smiled and said, "Of course. We got this, little brother."

I was nine again, and my big sister was there to walk me home and to make certain no one messed with me. I wiped the tears from my eyes, smiled right back at her, and said, "Yeah, we got this."

The meeting with my attorney went smoothly. We discussed a few scenarios I could face in court and what our response would be with each possible situation. Even though my sister wasn't licensed in New York, it was very helpful having her legal input. The next few days leading up to court allowed my sister and me the opportunity to catch up and for me to not focus so heavily on the upcoming court date. We hung out like the old days. Our cousin, who lives in New Jersey, joined us on a few occasions. Having my family with me gave me strength. I needed their support. I was also excited I could formally introduce my big sister to Anyanwu. We all hung out the weekend before Monday's court hearing and had a great time. Afterwards, my big sister said I seemed very happy with Anyanwu and she with me. She said it was good to finally see me truly happy.

The next day, we all went to church—my sister, my cousin, and my mother. My mother had come back recently from Atlanta to be with me during this time. She promised to stay until Kisha and I were re-united. Even though I had tried to shield my family from my domestic struggles, as many men in my situation do, I was eternally thankful for their support at this moment. We prayed and listened to gospel music together that Sunday morning. The preacher's powerful words of faith and redemption and the hopeful spirit that permeated church were cathartic. I sang, cried, and prayed hard that day. I was ready. It was time to go and be reunited with my daughter.

CHAPTER EIGHT

FAMILY COURT

Standing in front of a judge again was as unnerving as the first time, but I felt more confident than I had in domestic court. I was ready to get this started; I wanted to see my daughter again.

Before we started, the judge made an announcement. She proclaimed she'd previously been a part of a legal project with the head of Katherine's attorney's law firm. Even though their respective roles hadn't caused them to have much contact, she wanted me to know this and for me to decide if she should recuse herself from the case. This recusal would cause the case to be delayed, which meant more time away from my child. She allowed me a moment to confer with my attorney. Outside the courtroom, I huddled with my "legal team": my attorney, my sister, my mother, my cousin, and my father. Anyanwu was there, but she remained in another part of the courthouse until the proceeding concluded. I wanted Anyanwu in the courtroom, but my attorney felt it best if she wasn't there. She said it could unnecessarily provoke Katherine.

In the huddle, everyone offered thoughts on what should happen. My mother and cousin wanted a new judge. They believed this judge would probably be biased against me. My father agreed. My attorney said that on the one hand, proceeding with this judge could be risky; on the other hand, she could go out of her way to avoid bias.

I looked over at my big sister. She hadn't offered her opinion yet. She was quiet for a moment. "What do you want to do?" she asked.

I lowered my head and said a quiet prayer. When I finished, I looked up and said, "Let's go back in. We're doing this now."

The judge started with the domestic violence matter, which had been sent over to her. My attorney laid out my case first. Yolanda called no witnesses. She spoke directly from my deposition. Everything she needed to say was already there. As she spoke, I looked back and forth at my ex, her attorney, and the judge. Her attorney didn't object to what Yolanda was presenting, and my ex became agitated. The judge calmly listened.

After Yolanda concluded, it was time for Katherine's attorney. He stumbled through a few retorts to what Yolanda had presented. Once more, his counterargument didn't match his expensive attire. He seemed unsure of what he wanted to say. After speaking for a moment, he called me to the stand. As I walked up towards the stand, I looked back at my family. Seeing them there was comforting. Katherine's attorney asked me a few clarifying questions, such as when Katherine and I had met and how long we'd been together before our child's birth. Katherine interrupted. She wanted to speak with her attorney. The judge allowed it. Katherine's facial expression indicated she wasn't pleased with her attorney's line of questioning. They went back and forth for a couple of minutes. The judge's patience grew thin. She ordered the attorney to continue. He asked me one further question: "Do you know anything about paint thinner?"

Katherine had alleged in her domestic violence report that I'd recklessly exposed Kisha and her (Katherine's) aunt to paint thinner fumes while I was painting the kitchen. I told the attorney no, that did not happen. He didn't ask any follow-up questions. Katherine was visibly agitated at her attorney's lack of aggressive questioning. Yolanda didn't bother to cross-examine me. The judge asked if there were any more witnesses. Katherine's attorney hesitated before saying, "Yes, my client's daughter, Your Honor."

Katherine was prepared to place our daughter on the stand to testify against me. This deeply saddened and angered me. I looked over at Yolanda. She sensed my level of frustration and quickly objected. The judge shared my concern. She asked the attorney if he was seriously considering placing a young child on the stand. The attorney again hesitated. "Yes, Your Honor, that's correct." I wanted to cry at this point. I couldn't stomach the idea of my daughter sitting on the stand being questioned by this attorney about anything related to this matter. I looked over at Katherine, hoping she'd see my hurt and know that she'd gone too far. Thankfully, the judge didn't allow my daughter as a witness. She said she wouldn't permit a young child to experience such a frightening moment. She added that she was shocked Katherine and her attorney thought this was a viable option and questioned the overall motives of a parent who would suggest such a thing.

With no further witnesses or testimony, the judge ruled. The domestic violence case was without merit and would therefore be dismissed. She said there would be a forty-five-minute recess before she heard the custody portion of our case. Outside the courtroom I started to cry. No more domestic violence madness to contend with. I was one step closer to seeing my daughter again. My family hugged one another in celebration. They wanted to go upstairs to the courthouse cafeteria for quick refreshments. I decided to stay by the courtroom and wait.

Anyanwu was already in the courthouse eating area awaiting the end of the court appearance. Even though it was strategically decided she wouldn't be in the courtroom, she wanted to be there to support me. I wanted that as well. Not knowing what was happening in the courtroom was unnerving for her. Our feelings for each other had deepened, and we'd grown extremely close. I appreciated her support and understanding.

Anyanwu saw my family enter the eating area. Katherine's family was already there. Kisha was with her maternal aunt. Anyanwu witnessed Kisha's excited reaction as she saw my sister enter the lunch area. Kisha must have thought I was there too. I knew she missed me. It had now been about two months since my daughter and I had last seen each other. Thankfully, her aunt briefly allowed my daughter to say hello to my sister and the rest of my family. Anyanwu saw my daughter's expression dampen somewhat when she did not see me, but Kisha was still glad to see her father's family.

Going back into the courtroom was no less unnerving than an hour before. Even though the judge had dismissed the domestic violence matter, we still needed to resolve the custody issue. Before starting the custody hearing, the judge asked if we'd already gone to mediation. We had in fact attended mediation. Mediation was required before all family court matters. It allowed the two opposing parties the opportunity to work out a solution before appearing before the judge. Typically, the two parties attended mediation together, but because our case involved domestic violence charges, we met with the mediator separately. Because I was the plaintiff, I saw the mediator first. This was the first time I'd personally told my truth in a court-related setting. Yolanda was my voice in the courtroom; in mediation, I was speaking for myself. I had to balance my hurt and my frustration. I couldn't let my frustration override my ability to discuss the history of the case and then offer a workable solution that Katherine would embrace.

I was with the mediator for about fifteen to twenty minutes. Afterwards, Katherine met with the mediator. They met for almost forty minutes before the mediator emerged from the room. The mediator said Katherine had rejected my solution, which was joint legal custody (where we would equally make decisions about doctors, schools, and other important life matters) and shared physical custody. Katherine's solution was full physical and legal custody for her and twice-weekly visits for me. I rejected her offer. The mediator said she sensed that Katherine was emotionally unbalanced and, in her opinion, was operating from a place of anger and not in the best interest of the child. Unfortunately, all the mediator could report was that there was no mutually agreed-upon solution. Yolanda reported this to the judge, and the hearing resumed.

Yolanda presented first. She laid out a strong argument. It boiled down to this: I was a good father who wanted to have a relationship with his child, uninterrupted by false allegations. Katherine's attorney attempted to re-present the allegations from the domestic violence matter. The judge didn't allow that. She reminded him she'd already decided on that matter. With the domestic violence piece removed, Katherine's attorney had very little weight remaining in his argument. He basically said my ex wanted full physical and legal custody because I was an irresponsible father. The judge asked me directly what I'd presented in mediation. I told her about my plan for joint physical and legal custody, that I'd like the custody to be a week with me and a week with Katherine. The judge said she was not inclined to agree, and my heart froze. She quickly explained she wasn't inclined to allow such a young child to be removed from a home she knew so well and placed in a week on/week off arrangement, but perhaps when Kisha got a little older it could be allowed. For now, the judge would permit shared legal custody and a fair visitation schedule.

Katherine didn't look happy about this. She said something to her attorney, and her attorney objected. The judge asked on what basis.

The attorney said his client believed I'd deliberately attempt to sabotage all legal decisions regarding the child to "get back" at her for filing the domestic violence charges. The judge overruled the objection. The judge proceeded to outline our new agreement. I'd get three days a week from after school until 8:00 p.m. and one overnight every other week. We'd rotate holidays and have shared legal custody. Lastly, all pickups and drop-offs would be done at a police station close to the child's home. The judge did this to avoid the possibility of problems during the exchanges. That day would have been one of my visit days, so Yolanda asked if I could get my daughter then and bring her back at the appointed time. The judge said yes. I grew weak. I'd finally get to see my daughter again. I was overwhelmed with happiness.

Outside the courtroom, Katherine's attorney approached me and shook my hand. My ex had already gone upstairs to get our daughter. Her attorney told me I seemed like a very good man and father, and he hated meeting me under these circumstances. I appreciated his openness.

My mind reeled from the court experience. I hugged all my family members as well as my attorney. I profusely thanked her for all her hard work and courtroom acumen. Then the elevator door opened, and I saw my daughter. It was like a movie. Katherine was holding her hand and trying to tell her something, but when my daughter saw me, she released herself from Katherine's hand and ran over to me. She jumped into my arms, and I held her as if it were the first time I'd seen her years ago at the hospital. We both cried. Kisha told me she'd missed me and heartwarmingly tapped my nose and said, "I love you, Daddy."

I had my baby back.

***

"Monkey Man," I called as she stood by the dessert bar. "You must eat your dinner first, baby girl, before you have dessert."

I was so excited to have Kisha back, I almost let her have the dessert. My heart was filled with happiness as my daughter and I walked back over to the table to join the rest of my family, including Anyanwu and her son. This was the first time my daughter met Anyanwu and her child. Anyanwu and I had made the decision it was best to make introductions when the time was right. Well, the time was right. We described our relationship to her son, Tyson, and Kisha as a friendship. We wanted to give them time to adjust to all the changes happening in their lives before letting them know we were more than friends. This entire moment seemed surreal. Deep down I always believed I'd get my daughter back into my life; however, after nearly two months of waiting, my faith had been tested. Still, here we all were, celebrating the return of my daughter.

"Thank you, Lord, for bringing my granddaughter back to us," said my mother as she led us in prayer. "Thank you for the blessing of family, and thank you for the continued hedge of protection over my son, his daughter, and the entire family. Amen."

"Amen!" Kisha screamed out. We all laughed. As we ate, shared family memories, and ate some more, I thought to myself, *This is a good day.*

CHAPTER NINE

CHILD PROTECTIVE SERVICES

There are moments in your life that you never forget. For me, this phone call would be one of those unforgettable moments.

"Marvin, this is Wendy calling from the Office of Child and Family Services [OCFS]. You got a moment?"

"Sure. What can I do for you Wendy?"

"I need to discuss the new allegations."

Allegations? I was so shaken; I did not hear the word new. I had already discussed the allegations of domestic violence and child endangerment the first time Wendy came to my home shortly after the domestic court hearing.

That first time I met with Wendy, my plan was to show her I wasn't the man she'd read about in her reports because I wasn't that man. The first thing I did before we engaged in dialogue about the allegations was to read her a passage from Kahlil Gibran's *The Collected Works*. The passage was about parenting. Anyanwu didn't want me to do this. She thought it would backfire somehow. The poem speaks of a mother's yearning to know the true purpose of parenthood. It reads:

And a Woman who held a babe against her bosom said, Speak to us of Children.

And he said:

Your children are not your children. They are the sons and daughters of Life's longing for itself. They come through you but not from you, and though they are with you yet they belong not to you.

You may give them your love but not your thoughts, for they have their own thoughts. You may house their bodies but not their souls. . . .

You are the bows from which your children as living arrows are sent forth. The archer sees the mark upon the path of the infinite, and He bends you with His might that His arrows may go swift and far. Let your bending in the archer's hand be for gladness; For even as He loves the arrow that flies, so He loves also the bow that is stable.

"This poem is how I view parenting," I told Wendy. She looked at me a moment before speaking. I'm certain she had read her report before meeting me, a report that contained a very different picture of the man who sat in front of her now. She said that she loved Kahlil Gibran. She had a few of his pieces read at her wedding. I was no longer some anonymous, alleged perpetrator of domestic violence. I was a human being, a caring father sitting before her. Now we could talk.

A couple of weeks after that initial meeting, Wendy called me and said that the case was closed because the allegations were "unsubstantiated," so I was confused by this call. "I thought the case was closed," I said.

"These are new allegations," Wendy repeated.

I took a deep breath. I wanted to hang up and pretend this moment wasn't happening. "What allegations?"

She informed me that additional claims of abuse had come through the OCFS child abuse hotline, conveniently a few days after Katherine had questioned our daughter and discovered that she'd been to Anyanwu's home and had dinner.

There was no end to this. I couldn't stop this volcano from erupting.

"More allegations! What the hell are they talking about, Marvin?" The hurt and anger in Anyanwu's voice reverberated like thunder through the phone.

I wanted to say something comforting, but I couldn't think of anything. All I could offer was a simple, "I'll take care of this."

Those words did not suffice. Anyanwu wanted details. She needed real answers.

"All I know is that OCFS received a tip that Kisha was abused when she came over to your home."

"That is simply not true!!!" Anyanwu continued, "The kids played and had fun that night. This is nothing but more of her lies." Anyanwu grew increasingly more frustrated as she spoke. "It wasn't enough that she got your daughter removed from your life for over two months; now she is trying to jeopardize my career and possibly my entire life as well!"

The OCFS worker called Anyanwu mid-conversation. "I have an unlisted number calling me," said Anyanwu. "Could that be OCFS?"

I told Anyanwu most likely yes, and if she didn't want to accept the call, she didn't have to until I got more details. Anyanwu wasn't one to walk away from a difficult situation. She accepted the call using her three-way feature so I could listen silently.

"Anyanwu, I am with OCFS. Do you have a moment?"

"Yes, what can I do for you?"

"There have been allegations that you physically abused Kisha when she was at your home last week. Were you alone with the child at all during the time she was in your home that night?"

"No. We watched television for a while—Kisha, my son, and Marvin. Afterwards, Kisha and my son played a bit in my son's room while Marvin and I watched a little more TV. Then Marvin took Kisha home. I'm not certain if you see it or not, but there's a very dangerous pattern emerging here. If you look closely at the brief history of this case, this woman's allegations against her child's father have escalated rapidly. The first allegations were domestic abuse and child neglect. These charges were heard in two courts, and both found them to have no merit. OCFS couldn't substantiate the domestic abuse charges, and now these allegations. This woman is not only trying to disrupt Marvin's relationship with his daughter; now she's trying to damage mine. Has OCFS had an opportunity to review the court records yet?"

"No, but we have requested a copy and should have them very soon."

"I will make myself available to whatever investigation OCFS wants to have, and I am 100 percent confident that after all the facts have been properly obtained and reviewed in this matter, it will be closed as unsubstantiated."

The call seemed to take forever. Anyanwu said she was comfortable with how the call ended. I reassured her that I'd do everything I could to make certain that OCFS closed this matter quickly and quietly as an unsubstantiated matter.

Two days later, as I left church with Kisha, she told me her mother had questioned her repeatedly about the playdate and told her to say things to the school and therapist. Katherine had secured the services of a therapist when the restraining order was active. I could have requested a new therapist once I got joint legal custody; however, I did not want to create more disruptions in Kisha's life.

The next morning, I called Kisha's therapist. I had had the opportunity to speak with the therapist once before to give details of my daughter's paternal history. I knew that if the therapist was going to provide effective treatment, she'd need a balanced account of my daughter's paternal history. Before I could get into the conversation with the therapist, she told me she had been planning to call me to let me know that based upon her last session with Kisha, she was compelled to make a report with OCFS.

I paused for a second. I needed a moment to compose myself. I asked if it was my ex or my daughter who had made the disclosure. The therapist said my ex was in the room and had prompted my daughter in the beginning of the disclosure to tell what had happened. I couldn't believe what I was hearing. I reminded the therapist about the contentious relationship between Katherine and me, and I asked why she hadn't contacted me to get my understanding of the situation before contacting OCFS. The therapist said that she was mandated to report suspected child abuse, not to investigate it. She said that she had planned to call me that morning. I was too angry to continue the call. I did not want that anger to filter into my conversation with the therapist. I thanked the therapist and told her we'd speak later. This wasn't good. It was one thing if Katherine had made the call to OCFS, but my daughter's therapist was on another level of urgency. I felt exhausted and weak.

I called the worker from OCFS to get an understanding of what the investigation would look like. The OCFS worker told me that due to the nature of the case, it would be more involved than the last investigation. She explained that OCFS would have to speak with staff from my daughter's school, Katherine, me, perhaps Anyanwu, maybe Anyanwu's son because he was there the night in question, Kisha's therapist, and certain maternal family members. The OCFS worker also said this could lead to a police investigation.

My next visit with Kisha was very difficult. I was nervous. I wasn't angry or disappointed with her. I'm not certain if she understood the severity of this matter. I didn't want her to know. It was difficult to hide my emotions, but it was my responsibility to keep her shielded from these issues. So I smiled through my worry and dismay, and I had the best time I could with her. The nervousness remained because OCFS was back in my relationship with my daughter. I had to closely monitor every word I said in front of Kisha. I didn't make it a habit to speak inappropriately around her; however, with this intense spotlight on me, I couldn't make any mistakes. I was imprisoned, with limited ability to have any type of a normal relationship with my daughter.

As days progressed and the investigation proceeded, this nervousness slowly morphed into paranoia. I became excessively guarded about what anyone would say or do around my daughter. This included my mother. I wouldn't permit my mother to verbally correct my daughter when she'd done something wrong. I couldn't risk anything questionable being said or done in front of my daughter and my daughter telling Katherine, who would mischaracterize things to OCFS.

This effort to control everything and everyone when my daughter was present was unnerving and humiliating. Additionally, having to isolate my family from her was not easy or fair. I knew they loved her very much, but losing my daughter again terrified me. I needed to monitor all conversations and interactions around her. I wouldn't allow anything to be said or done that could be misinterpreted. I felt that my autonomy as a father was slowly evaporating into OCFS's hands.

This went on for weeks until I received a call from the OCFS worker informing me that after an extensive investigation, the matter would be closed and classified as unsubstantiated. She cautioned me that if any further allegations were made, OCFS would red-flag the case file, and the outcome could be very different. She said her supervisor wanted to meet with Katherine and me to admonish us both to resolve this custody dispute in a more amicable fashion that didn't involve OCFS. The meeting was set for the coming week. Relief flooded my mind. OCFS was no longer pursuing the erroneous abuse allegations, but I still needed to talk about what I was feeling and experiencing.

I decided to visit the father's group again. I hadn't been since the first time I attended. That had been a mistake. Being with those other fathers allowed me to share my experience in a way that I couldn't with any others during this time. As close as I was to my family and Anyanwu, it was difficult to elicit the advice or suggestions I needed to hear because they'd never experienced this dynamic in their own parenting experiences.

In the father's group, I didn't speak at first; I listened and observed. There were many of the same fathers who had been there the first time I had attended and some new faces. What wasn't new were the rules. No bad-/foul-talking about your child's mother. No projecting blame onto others. Most importantly, be honest and accountable. The first time I'd attended, following all these rules wasn't easy, especially the one about not bad-talking your child's mother. This time was even harder. I'd been through two court hearings and two OCFS investigations, and I suspected more drama to follow. I related all this chaos directly to Katherine's thoughtless actions, but the honest and accountable fathers in the room reminded me that Katherine hadn't forced me into a relationship. I had made the choice to enter and remain in this dysfunction. Truth was, Katherine hadn't forced me to remain in the relationship when the relationship had clearly declined. I had chosen to stay over and over, mostly out of fear of losing contact with my child and, if I am being honest, because I was comfortable with dysfunction.

One father said, "You can waste energy and time hating your child's mother, and some of those feelings may be understandable—hell, even justified—but those feelings will not bring you any closer to your child or children. Those feelings will not end an OCFS case or get a judge to sympathize with you. Choose love." He paused and looked around at every father in the room. "All of you sitting around this room today must love your child more than you hate your circumstances with your child's mother. I don't care what those circumstances are—false OCFS allegations and police reports; long, drawn-out court battles; or being denied the right to see your child for weeks, months, or even years. Loving your children will be the fuel you need to get through another day, get through another court hearing, another OCFS investigation, another moment when you feel like the entire world is against you. Most importantly, loving your child will be what he or she needs to get through this storm, a storm that they didn't create."

The next day I picked Kisha up for our visit. As I watched her play joyfully and innocently in the sandbox, I reflected on the words shared by that father: "Love your child. Love your child more than you hate the circumstances." So I did that. I put down all the thoughts about OCFS, courts, and all the things connected with those situations and learned to appreciate every second I had with my daughter. It turned out to be a tremendous day. We played Free the Princess from the Witch's Dungeon, Lost Ship on the Ocean, and so many other wonderful pretend games; then we laughed and shared jokes and funny stories at dinner. My daughter seemed very happy. I vowed to try my best to live in a moment of love every time we had a visit. I knew this wouldn't be possible all the time, but she deserved nothing less.

As I dropped my daughter off back at the castle (that's what I chose to call the police station to help her not see it as a bad thing), I was both sad and happy—sad because we had to say our "see you later" (I made it a habit of not saying goodbye to her after our long, forced separation) and because she had to experience a childhood of courts and police stations; but happy because I didn't allow all this madness to prevent me from having a really good day with my daughter.

CHAPTER TEN

TURNING TIDES

On the day I was scheduled to meet with the OCFS supervisor, I was surprisingly happy. The visit with my daughter the day before had gone well, I'd reconnected with my fatherhood group, and the abuse allegations had been found to be unsubstantiated. Anyanwu was asked to attend the meeting with me.

When we arrived at the OCFS offices, we were greeted with a surprise. Katherine wasn't at the meeting as planned. Instead the OCFS supervisor reported to us that Katherine was at the police station filing abuse charges against us. The supervisor further disclosed that Katherine had filed a complaint with his own supervisor against him and the OCFS worker for their failure to properly protect our daughter. The OCFS supervisor said the complaint wouldn't alter their previous decision; the allegations would remain unsubstantiated. The supervisor further explained that OCFS's final decision on the abuse charges wouldn't prevent the police from acting against us if their investigation warranted such action. The supervisor suggested we go down to the police station and discuss the matter.

During the car ride to the station, Anyanwu and I were quiet. We drove and listened to the radio. We called no one. Before exiting the vehicle, we said a short prayer and hugged. As we walked into the police station, we saw Katherine and Kisha talking with a woman police officer. Kisha saw us first. She joyfully screamed out, "Daddy and Ms.

Anyanwu!" When Katherine saw us, she hurried our daughter into a room close by. We walked over to the officer Katherine had just spoken with and introduced ourselves. The officer looked shocked. She asked us to have a seat, and she'd have another officer speak with us. Waiting for that other officer seemed like an eternity. My mind raced. Would Anyanwu and I be arrested? Would this arrest occur while Kisha was still there? The knots in my stomach grew tighter by the second.

Finally, two officers emerged from another room beyond the front desk. They came over and introduced themselves. We greeted the officers nervously. The lead officer thanked us for coming down so quickly and then detailed the complaint that had been lodged against us. As he spoke, I saw Kisha playing in the room through the double-paned windows. She was oblivious to what was happening. All she knew, I assumed and hoped, was that her mother had taken her to the castle where the exchanges occurred. Perhaps she thought she was there to meet me. After sharing our version of what had occurred the night in question and the weeks following, I asked the officers what would happen now. The officer said we could relax. If they had thought we'd abused my daughter, we'd have been in handcuffs already. The officers also said Katherine had been to the station two or three times prior to this, attempting to file charges against us, and each time she came, the allegations grew more serious.

The officer said that we were free to go but also that we'd most likely be contacted by a police investigator, as was protocol in these types of matters. He said the investigator would most likely want to get an official statement from Anyanwu, Katherine, me, and even Kisha. The nightmare seemed like it would never end. However, I was thankful we were walking out of the police station and headed home.

The next day, I received a phone call from the OCFS supervisor. He said he'd rescheduled the visit that had been canceled due to Katherine's nonappearance and expected to see the three of us in his office that coming Thursday. He said Katherine had already committed to being there. I assured him I'd be there as well. I wondered if Katherine would show or if she would have another surprise waiting for me. I tried to stay positive, but the continual landslide of gloom connected to this matter seemed never-ending.

That night, I picked up Kisha from the castle for our regular visit. Neither she nor I mentioned the police station incident from the day before. We laughed and played as if all were normal in our world. Perhaps between the two of us, it was normal. I was happy to have my daughter with me, and she was happy to have her dad. Before dropping her off, she reminded me of the event at her school the next day. Even though it was not my regular visit day, I'd made a habit of attending all her school events, and this one was no different. I promised her I'd be there. I knew Katherine would be there as well. However, that wouldn't stop me from supporting my daughter as her father.

I arrived at the school as they were setting up for the event and helped the staff set up the chairs. Afterwards, the principal asked if she could speak with me briefly. She asked me how things were between Katherine and me. She seemed deeply concerned. She revealed to me that Katherine had asked her if Kisha had said anything negative to her about me or my girlfriend. Katherine also reminded the principal that if Kisha had said something, that as a mandated reporter, she was obligated to report it. The principal told me she couldn't understand why Katherine was asking her this until the OCFS worker came to the school and talked to her. I told the principal OCFS had closed the matter as an unsubstantiated allegation. The principal also said

Katherine had told the school they should no longer use my last name on any school documents, only her last name. She asked me if this was correct. I told the principal my daughter's legal last name was still mine, and that hadn't been changed in any court proceeding. I was glad I had the opportunity to clarify those things with the principal. I was exceedingly happier when my daughter stepped into the room with the rest of her class to begin their singing performance.

My daughter was very excited when she saw me. Her voice seemed to rise above all her classmates. By that time, Kathrine had arrived at the school. We saw each other but exchanged no words. After the performance, my daughter ran over to me and gave me a giant hug. She said she was so glad I could make it. We sat, talked, and ate cookies together. I saw Katherine standing over by the door, waiting for Kisha to return to her. She called for Kisha to come to her. I didn't want to create a scene, so I told my daughter to go over to her mother, and I'd see her tomorrow at the castle for our visit.

As I got up to leave, my daughter jumped into my arms to give me a final goodbye hug. That obviously irritated Katherine, which was not my intention. She quickly walked over to me and began pulling our daughter from my arms. Kisha held me tighter. I told her to go with Mommy and begged Katherine to give her a moment to get down, but she refused. She yelled, "Give me my daughter, you fucking child abuser!"

Several parents looked in disbelief at what they'd just witnessed. I quickly gave my daughter to my ex and exited the school. I immediately called and reported the incident to the social worker. I didn't want her to hear about this matter from anyone else. It was nerve-racking enough being under OCFS's relentless watchful eye; now I didn't want to provide them with a reason to intensify their surveillance of me or my relationship with my daughter.

Don't get me wrong; this is not an indictment of the entire OCFS system. They provide good services when needed. But I didn't need or want their services to invade my life any further. The OCFS worker thanked me for the call and said she would notify her supervisor immediately.

The next day, I received a call from the OCFS worker informing me that her supervisor wanted to see me and Katherine in OCFS offices the day after next. I contacted my attorney to apprise her of the meeting and asked if she should attend. We agreed that I should attend without counsel and call her if necessary. We didn't want to exacerbate the matter by involving legal support when it was not apparent such support was required. I called my older brother. He also agreed I should attend without counsel. He said the presence of an attorney could change the entire atmosphere of the meeting. The frightening thing was, I didn't know what the atmosphere of this meeting would be.

My work as a program director had brought me to OCFS offices many times. Each time I entered their offices, I entered with confidence. This time it was different. I was the parent facing the possibility of losing my child, not the confident family facilitator coming to the rescue of a parent like Superman bravely flying into a burning building. I was petrified. My fear stemmed from a feeling of helplessness. Even though I was doing everything possible to demonstrate to OCFS that I wasn't an irresponsible parent, I was still aware of the fact that they could determine my daughter was better off in foster care due to what was happening between Katherine and me, many times in front of our child. The parents with whom I worked had tried to describe this helpless feeling to me. I could never fully embrace or understand the degree of helplessness being described until this moment. The prospect of someone legally being able to take your child from you, the child you've loved all his or her life, is one of the most emotionally and mentally crippling feelings anyone can experience.

I saw the OCFS worker standing by the front desk as I entered. I walked over to her. She told me Katherine had arrived with her brother. The worker said Katherine was in tears and refused to attend the meeting without her brother present because she was "extremely afraid of me." The worker also told me Kisha was there. The worker asked if I had any objection to Katherine's brother attending the meeting. I said I didn't, but I didn't know my daughter would be a part of this meeting. The worker assured me Kisha wouldn't attend; she'd be in a playroom out of sight of the meeting room.

The meeting room was populated by the OCFS worker, her supervisor, a Department of Mental Health (DMH) psychologist, an OCFS meeting facilitator, me, Katherine, and her brother. As with all OCFS meetings, the facilitator opened the meeting with an overview of what had brought the family to the attention of OCFS and a list of strengths of the family and child provided by all meeting attendees. Even though I knew the drill from my professional experiences, each moment of the meeting was like a horror movie as I sat frightfully awaiting the monster to jump out and strike. When it was my turn to speak, I'd carefully listened to and considered every word I'd heard. I didn't want to take a wrong turn with my words and come face to face with my worst fears – losing my daughter. We discussed many deeply personal things concerning my relationship with Katherine, our ongoing failed parenting dynamic, and how this dynamic was negatively affecting Kisha. It was humiliating and frustrating to have to disclose such personal information with a roomful of virtual strangers.

The topic turned to the subject of the recent school performance where Katherine had publicly screamed those obscene words at me in front of Kisha. The supervisor spoke first. He directed his comment to me.

"Please clarify the details of the school event."

I explained what had happened. The supervisor's demeanor became foreboding as he asked Katherine if what I said about her screaming the grossly obscene words in front of the child was true. Katherine surprisingly didn't deny it. As she attempted to clarify the reasons she had chosen to speak those words, the supervisor interrupted her and said he had heard all he needed to hear, and based upon this and other recent occurrences, he no longer felt confident the child was safe in Katherine's care. The psychologist concurred, saying she found the mother's actions to be emotionally abusive to Kisha. The supervisor asked me if I was prepared to take the child home. I was confused, but I said yes.

Katherine's brother started crying and asked his sister what was happening. Katherine turned to her brother and said, "They are taking my child from me and giving her to Marvin." As I looked at Katherine robotically explaining to her brother what was unfolding, I couldn't help but notice that unlike her brother, she wasn't crying the way she had been outside the room prior to this meeting.

I didn't have time to ruminate on what her lack of tears meant because my thoughts quickly shifted back to what was occurring. Kisha was being removed from Katherine and conditionally placed under my care. Because Katherine was legally the custodial parent, OCFS's removal of Kisha from her care meant that our daughter was technically a ward of the state. This meant that if OCFS deemed it necessary, my daughter could be temporarily placed in a foster home pending a dependency court hearing, which would determine the most suitable long-term placement. In the interim, it was decided I'd be a suitable placement. This meant that I, her biological father, was the equivalent of a foster home placement.

I struggled to find the silver lining in this moment, but I couldn't. There wasn't a bright side to this situation. Even though Kisha was coming home with me, it wasn't permanent. OCFS was deeper in our life, and now we had to go to dependency court. Unlike family court, dependency court doesn't decide visitation schedules. This court determines whether a child should remain with his or her biological parent(s), go into the foster care system, or possibly be adopted by new parents.

That night I barely slept, thinking about all the worst-case scenarios that could occur in dependency court. The more I tried to suppress the vision of my daughter being torn from my arms and thrown into foster care, the stronger the thought emerged. Though I knew this wasn't quite how it happened in dependency court, my mind wouldn't stop processing in this distorted manner. I looked over at Kisha peacefully sleeping and cried at the thought of her waking up in a strange home with people she didn't know because her mother and father couldn't properly manage their parental responsibilities, their emotions. I fell asleep with a heavy heart.

The next morning, I awakened to a phone call from the OCFS worker. She called to inform me OCFS had arranged for Katherine to visit with Kisha at one of their offices starting the next day, and for Kisha's assured safety, this and all subsequent visits would be professionally monitored until dependency court determined otherwise.

The next day, I took Kisha to the OFCS location as directed. The monitored visit went without incident. Kisha didn't seem to notice she and her mother were being watched their entire visit, or at least she didn't mention anything to me about it afterwards. I guess she was just happy to see her mother. After the visit, the OCFS worker informed me the dependency court would start six days from that date. She said I'd be appointed a state-sponsored attorney if I didn't choose to hire a private attorney. I'd already spoken to Yolanda about representing me in dependency court. Unfortunately, dependency court was outside the scope of her practice, so she couldn't offer her services. I didn't want to go through the process of hiring a private attorney, nor did I have the means to do so. I still had Yolanda on retainer. So I'd be using a state attorney as many parents have done and continue to do, mostly due to financial constraints.

CHAPTER ELEVEN

DEPENDENCY COURT

It was three days away from dependency court. I was nervous and wanted to isolate myself until the day of, but I still had to work. In fact, I had a client appointment at the same dependency court I had to go to in three days.

I'd been to this court several times before to support my clients. This time was different. As I walked into the building, it appeared larger. It's funny how your perspective changes when you're on the other side of a situation. In my role as a program director, this court-house was a place of business. I came there to help parents keep their children or get them back. In three days, it would be my turn to be helped. Even going through the security checkpoint seemed to take longer than all the other times. I noticed each parent being checked thoroughly, as if they were there to do mischief. When I got to the courtroom floor, I greeted my client, and we talked a short moment.

Afterwards, I looked around the courtroom floor at all the people waiting their turn to present their respective cases in front of the judge. I never realized how unhappy and defeated these parents looked until this moment. I felt sad and ashamed—sad because I knew many of these parents would leave the court without a victory, and that meant not getting their child back or losing their child. A few would leave empty-handed because they were legitimately not ready to have their child or children back in their primary care, others because of poor legal representation, and some due to their diminishing willpower to continue fighting an intense court battle. I was ashamed because it took personally going through this situation to open my eyes to the pain of these parents. I was a good parental advocate. I fought hard to keep families together. However, I'd been fighting with my mind and neglecting to fully engage my heart. That would change.

It was two days from dependency court, and I still hadn't spoken with my court-appointed lawyer. I'd called five times without a return call. I was anxious and irritated. I finally told the lawyer's assistant that if I didn't hear from him within an hour, I'd report him to the court. Twenty minutes later he called. He wasn't happy, and I didn't care. I had too many questions to be answered. The first and most important question was, what was going to happen with my daughter? Would she stay with me, would she be going back with my ex, or worse, could she end up in foster care? The court lawyer avoided answering those questions. He instead chose to reprimand me for my "excessive calling." He apparently didn't appreciate my strong self-advocacy. Again, this didn't concern me. For me what was important at that moment was for him to know I was a parent who loved his daughter and wouldn't settle for subpar representation.

The lawyer told me calling multiple times wouldn't get me a return call any quicker. He said I should call once, and if he wasn't immediately available, I should leave a message and await his return call. I told him if he was too busy to communicate with me in a timely manner and, moreover, too impatient to deal with my type of parental advocacy, I could request the services of a new attorney. There was an awkward pause. The court lawyer then said he wasn't trying to dismiss my need to know what was going on with the case. He said right now my name was golden in the dependency report prepared by OCFS, and it was his job to keep it that way. I didn't say anything further. I'd been heard. I wanted this to be over. The court lawyer wasn't like my family court attorney, and I had to accept that. He wouldn't return my calls right away, but this was less important to me than my name remaining in good standing with OCFS. If my court lawyer could help achieve this, he didn't have to return any of my calls.

The next day came quickly. It was finally time for dependency court. I didn't want to go, but I had to. I didn't want to be called to the stand as a witness, but I had been issued a subpoena from Katherine's attorney as a potential witness. I was sick of the courts and police investigations. In fact, I had an appointment scheduled with a police detective the following week. I was totally over all the OCFS workers invading my privacy. I must have met with dozens of OCFS workers over the prior week. One OCFS worker even came to my house the day my daughter was released to me to make certain my home was suitable for my own daughter. I never took the time to truly imagine how degrading this must have felt to all the parents I'd represented over the years. Empathizing with the many parents who had to endure this stinging humiliation made the pain more hurtful. I was exhausted trying to have a normal relationship with my daughter under such abnormal circumstances. I didn't want to engage in this circus any longer. Whatever the reason, I didn't want to be there.

I saw my lawyer walking my way. I watched him as I entered the courtroom floor, but I didn't acknowledge him because he was talking to another parent, and I was too busy looking around the courthouse floor, hoping not to see any of my coworkers. I had done a good job keeping this matter from my employer. I'd disclosed what was occurring to only a select few. I didn't want to become the hot topic of office gossip. When I finally approached my lawyer, his greeting was more pleasant than our first encounter. Perhaps our talk had made a morsel of difference.

"The judge hearing this case today is tough but fair," my lawyer explained. "The mother's attorney is a powerhouse, very skilled with litigating these types of cases. The good news is, as I told you before, your name isn't mentioned in a negative way once in the report, and the DCFS attorneys and your daughter's attorney are very strong lawyers."

"So you, the OCFS attorneys, and my daughter's attorney will be working together?" I asked.

"No. We represent different interests. I'm representing your interest, your daughter's attorney is representing her interest, and the OCFS attorneys are representing OCFS's interest. There will be times throughout the court proceeding when those interests align because collectively we want to see the best outcome for your daughter."

"What outcome is that?" I asked.

"To make certain your daughter resides in a safe and nurturing home. Currently, OCFS has determined your residence is that home."

The case was called over the loudspeaker. It was time. I looked over at Katherine and her family and friends, who were assembled by the courtroom door. There must have been over twenty people present supporting her. Many of them I recognized. They formed a huge circle around her and prayed. As they went to enter the courtroom, the court officer stopped them and announced only Katherine could enter. As I walked past them, they stared at me with anger and disapproval. I assumed Katherine had convinced them this horrible moment was my fault and I was the reason she and Kisha had been separated. As hurtful as that thought was, I couldn't let it distract me. I had to remain mentally present while in the courtroom.

This particular courtroom was one I'd never entered. It looked like all the other dependency courtrooms I'd seen when I accompanied families. The familiar smell and dull white walls made me feel both welcomed and estranged. I sat next to my attorney. Kisha's lawyer and OCFS's attorneys all sat on my right, and Katherine and her attorney sat to my left. My seating arrangement, in the middle of all the other attorneys and directly in front of the judge, made me feel as if I were going to be the focal point of today's hearing.

The court officer said, "All rise to be sworn in."

It was go time.

***

Katherine's attorney had the floor first. Her first witness was Kisha's therapist. With each question, it didn't take long for me to accept that this lawyer was as good as my attorney had claimed. She was detailed, methodical, and very sharply dressed. Katherine must have paid a great deal of money for her services. Neither my attorney nor the other attorneys present objected much to her questions. After the attorney finished her line of questioning, there was a very brief cross-examination. Then the therapist was dismissed from the witness chair.

Over the next few hours, there were at least two additional witnesses. Because so many attorneys were attached to this case, the day was filled with objection after objection, sidebars, and multiple requests for the stenographer to do a read-back of a response not properly understood. It felt like an eternity. Finally, the judge adjourned for the day. Outside the court, my attorney said that it hadn't been the best day we could have had in there, but not to worry. He still felt strongly that things would end well.

"What does that mean, 'end well'?" I asked.

He reiterated, "Keep your name clean."

Because Kisha now lived with me full time, I had to enroll her in a school. She was still a ward of the state and would remain labeled as such until the court matter was resolved. Therefore, I had to obtain permission from her social worker to enroll her in a school close to my home. I felt like a person trying to parent from prison; however, I was determined not to let my mind become completely shackled in chains of fear and doubt. I continued following protocol. I didn't want to rock any unnecessary boats.

The school I had identified wasn't my daughter's assigned school. I liked the school because it was a magnet program. I called the school to see what I needed to do to enroll Kisha. I was informed that the school was filled, and there was a waiting list. I decided to go to the school and present my case. I thought honesty was the best policy. When I arrived at the school, there was one woman in the office. She didn't have the most approachable look; nonetheless, I didn't have time to waste.

"Hello, my name is Marvin, and this is my daughter, Kisha. I need a good school for her. She recently came to live with me, and I want her to be in a safe and productive school environment."

As I spoke, I became overwhelmed with emotion. I couldn't contain my tears. I promised my daughter would do her best there, and I'd be the type of parent who got involved in the school. I just needed some compassion. The office administrator took a moment to look over my daughter and me, then spoke directly to Kisha.

"Do you promise to do your best?"

"Yes, I will," Kisha said with her beautiful smile beaming throughout the room.

The office administrator looked back at me. "I'm going to help you get this baby into school. Bring her back this Monday, and she can start."

As I left the school, I called my mother and told her God had sent an angel to look out for us. My mother said it was great to know that my faith had not been broken. My faith was not broken, but truthfully, it was being tested like never before. I asked my mother to pray with me for my continued strength during this storm. She did. I love her prayers. I have always loved her prayers. They made me believe even when I wanted to give up. Now was one of those moments.

Having my daughter in a good school was a huge relief. I didn't have to worry about OCFS or any entity or person(s) questioning me about why my daughter wasn't in school yet. I needed to make certain I had covered all the required bases regarding my daughter, including up-to-date dentist and doctor visits, and of course school enrollment.

The first day at the new school was rough for my daughter. She was afraid to stay in her classroom and wanted to leave when I was leaving. She held my hand so tightly, I thought she'd break my fingers. The next day and the day after were easier for her. She came home a few days later talking and laughing about the friends she'd made. It was such a relief. It seemed all would be okay.

On my way to court, two weeks following my daughter starting her new school I received a call from my daughter's vice principal. The vice principal told me Kisha's mother had called the school, demanding to speak with the principal. Katherine told the vice principal Kisha should not be enrolled in that school. The vice principal said she was sorry, but she was going to have to disenroll my daughter from the school because she didn't want any trouble. I pleaded with the vice principal to delay her decision until I contacted Kisha's social worker. She gave me one hour. I called the OCFS worker and explained what was happening with the school. The OCFS worker did a three-way call and got my daughter's attorney on the phone. Kisha's attorney said she'd address this matter in court that same day. Afterwards, the OCFS worker called the school and spoke with the officer administrator. Thankfully, she was able to calm matters down, and my daughter remained in the school.

I was relieved for the moment but worried about the next land mine I'd encounter.

I went back to court after the school incident and tried to mentally prepare for the next round of witness testimonies. Before the next witness was called, Kisha's attorney approached the judge about the recent school matter and requested a stay-away order to keep Katherine from contacting or visiting Kisha's school. She explained the mother's actions to the court, including harassing the school staff, and how this had nearly resulted in the child being removed from the school. She explained that had it not been for the quick intervention of the social worker, Kisha's removal from her new school would have been permanent. Katherine's attorney objected to the request, but the judge granted a temporary stay-away order to last until the conclusion of the case.

It must have been devastating for Katherine. Even though I was pleased to know she couldn't negatively impact my daughter's school affairs, I was unhappy another wedge had been driven between Kisha and her mother. First the monitored visits, now this stay-away order—I was honestly sad for both. I wanted to freeze everyone in the courtroom except Katherine. In that frozen moment, I'd appeal to her to alter her course of action so we could come to one accord in our daughter's best interests. As my mind slipped deeper into this fantasy,

I was snapped back into reality by the court officer's loud call for the next witness to take the stand.

One day to the next, the trial continued. We were now in the sixth week of testimony. It was mentally exhausting to keep up with the different lines of questioning taking place in the courtroom. Five different attorneys and their constant barrage of questions and objections were overwhelming. This, in addition to keeping up primary care for a five-year-old child, was increasingly challenging and at times overwhelming.

I'd always been a dutiful father to my daughter. From her birth to that moment, I had never missed a day seeing her except when my court order visitation scheduled precluded me from visiting and during the restraining order period. On the days I didn't see her, I called her and said nightly prayers with her. We were very close. But her mother had provided the day-to-day hands-on care while I was at work. This was no longer the case. I was first at bat, and there were no other players on deck. It was sink or swim time, and sinking was not an option. Sinking meant Kisha would be left alone without either of her parents, and that would lead to our daughter being placed in foster care.

The first thing I had to get used to was cooking every night. For the first two weeks after Kisha came to live with me, we ate takeout or went to a restaurant. This habit became too expensive. The place I had secured after leaving my ex was a large one-bedroom apartment. It had a kitchen, but only a microwave and a stovetop. For me to make certain Kisha had well-balanced meals, I had to become creative with our meal selections. I started out cooking many pasta recipes. Once I learned how to properly utilize the stovetop, I introduced a variety of other meals that were as tasty as my pasta dishes but healthier . . . well, at least that is what Kisha told me.

Next I had to create a routine to get my daughter out of bed, cleaned, and dressed every day. I was now responsible for every aspect of her life, which included doing my best to shield her from the drama between her mother and me. I was determined to let my daughter have a normal five-year-old experience during a very unusual time.

As the weeks progressed, I shifted into a new parental space and state of mind. I felt more frustrated and fatigued than I had before taking on primary parental duties. At first I attributed the frustration to the court. We were now in our twelfth week with no end in sight. As exasperating and annoying as that was, I realized it wasn't completely litigation fatigue. I then thought it was the ongoing intrusion of OCFS in my life. I still had to meet with OCFS once weekly to give updates on my daughter's progress as well so she could have monitored visits with her mother. This was very taxing and embarrassing. I did not like walking into the OCFS offices with my daughter, but I couldn't attribute my frustration and fatigue solely to that.

It occurred to me that I was frustrated and fatigued because I was doing the work of two parents without a consistent support network. My mother had gone back to the East Coast, and over the past few weeks, Katherine's family had distanced themselves from Kisha. It was not from of a lack of love but more because they did not want to become embroiled too deeply in the ongoing court drama (or at least that is what I chose to believe). Anyanwu was supportive, but I didn't want to place my parental responsibility on her shoulders. My father and cousin were there for me, but day to day, it was pretty much Kisha and I.

One day I took Kisha to the park. Watching her joyfully play was a pleasure and relief. It was a relief because even though she was experiencing a new life, one without the presence of her mother, she remained high-spirited. Her enthusiasm was a source of inspiration for me. As she played, I noticed the other parents watching their children play. Ninety-five percent were mothers. Looking closer, I saw joy and deep fatigue written across their faces. The joy was already familiar to me, but now the fatigue was just as familiar. The fatigue and frustration I was beginning to experience were shared by so many mothers, both single and in committed relationships. In committed relationships like I'd been in with Katherine, the mother often shoulders most of the day-to-day parental duties, and the father often plays the supporting role. This is often the case even when both parents work full time.

My thoughts drifted to my mother. I thought about the sacrifices she had made over the years to facilitate a good life for my sister and me. She had done this without the accolades and praises that guys like me get, often from women, when they see a dad out with his children. My mother did what she had to do because if not her, then who? Most fathers know if they don't cook a meal, the mother will. They know if they don't make the child's lunch, help get them ready for school, or wash their clothes, the mother will be there to take care of it, as my mother did for her children. I called my mother later that night and said, "Thank you for loving us." I'm not certain she fully understood the reason for my call, but she deserved that thank-you, as do all the mothers who go the distance when no one else will.

We entered the eighteenth week of court. Many family members, friends, and professionals had been paraded on and off the witness stand, and it was now my turn. I was petrified. My attorney gave me two words of advice: *"Be honest."* Walking up to the stand felt different from the last time I had taken the stand in family court. The main difference was that Katherine's current attorney was much more forceful and thorough than her previous one. She was a well-dressed shark and skilled in these waters. The court officer reminded me I was still under oath. Then we started.

"When did you and Katherine meet?"

"Around June 2008 I responded.

"Were you married at the time?"

"Yes, I was."

"So, you started a relationship with Katherine knowing you were married and didn't tell her?"

I didn't answer. I waited a beat.

"Objection, leading," my attorney called out.

"Objection sustained." The judge replied.

The barrage of questions continued rapidly.

"Did you mislead Katherine about your marital status?"

"No, I didn't."

"Were you present when Anyanwu yelled at your daughter and pulled her arm?"

I didn't answer. Even though I wanted to, I looked at my attorney first. He quickly asserted his objection. "I object, Your Honor. Question assumes there was yelling and physical abuse."

"Objection sustained."

"Did Anyanwu yell at your daughter and pull her arm?"

"No, she did not." I answered.

As fast as I answered, the attorney presented me with the next question. I had spoken with my sister the day prior to my testimony. She had instructed me to do one important thing while testifying: answer only yes or no; don't offer any additional information. She warned me additional information could be used by the opposing attorney to surround me in a damaging narrative, a narrative built on a false premise. I remembered her advice as the attorney, and I continued our verbal jousting match.

"Were you and Katherine engaged to be married?"

"Yes." I responded.

"Did you ask her to marry you while you were still married?"

"No."

"So you weren't still married when you asked her to marry you?"

It was so tempting to expand on my answer. I wanted the full truth out there. However, my sister's admonishment rang loudly in my ears.

Thankfully, my attorney interjected. "Objection. My client already answered."

"Sustained."

I can't explain it. I'm not sure why, but as the questions continued, I became less and less nervous. I no longer needed to look at my attorney before answering; I just answered. Then it occurred to me why I was no longer nervous. I was operating out of truth and love. Yes, this attorney was skilled at making witnesses stumble over their words. The witness before me, an OCFS worker, had left the stand visibly frustrated because he'd been verbally tripped up several times. I knew the attorney's quick-wittedness and thorough line of questioning couldn't be taken for granted. I had to remain mentally vigilant but not nervous. I felt like Neo in the final scene of the first *Matrix* movie when he realized his full power. He saw the opposing force in their true form. He no longer needed to run from them. When I realized my truth and love for my daughter were the source of my power, I no longer felt nervous. I felt a power surge through my veins. I saw the attorney in her true form. She wasn't an unstoppable force I had to mentally flee; she was a human being like me, asking some questions.

As the line of questioning closed, I was exhausted. I was on the stand for nearly an hour, with only one short break. Afterwards, I talked briefly with my attorney.

"Was this your first time on a witness stand?" he asked.

"No," I replied. "I had to testify in family court, but it was nothing like this."

"Well, you did a great job. My only advice if you get called back up to the stand is to keep doing what you did before." I was relieved.

Later that evening I prepared dinner for Kisha and me. We sat alone in our apartment eating, laughing, and listening to Frank Sinatra. My daughter loved Ol' Blue Eyes, especially his tunes "New York, New York" and "The Girl from Ipanema." It was funny listening to Kisha sing the songs I'd introduced her to. Who would have thought a five-year-old would enjoy singing songs that were popular over forty and fifty years ago? As I looked at her singing and laughing, I wondered if she would remain this happy and carefree. Would she somehow overcome the challenges of a broken home and the intrusion of OCFS, police, and courts in her very young life? Maybe if all this worked out soon, it would slowly fade into the shadows of her subconscious, where it would seem like a bad dream. Maybe . . .

"Daddy! Why you stop singing?"

"Thanks, baby girl."

"For what, Daddy?"

"For bringing me back, baby girl." She smiled.

I know she didn't understand what I meant, but I was glad she had stopped me from crazy future thinking. It doesn't lead to anywhere productive. In fact, it only prevents one from enjoying the here and now. As Doris Day said, in her most popular song, "Que será, será/ Whatever will be, will be." What I needed to be right then was what Kisha needed most: an attentive, loving father.

The court hearing was slowly moving towards an end. We'd been through nearly six months of witness testimony. The last witness was scheduled to take the stand momentarily. It was Katherine. I was thankful this was concluding. Emotionally and socially, it had been exhausting and embarrassing. For example, for six grueling months, I had to duck and hide from potential coworkers. This court was one I and several of my coworkers frequented to support our clients in many different OCFS-related matters. Once I saw one of my coworkers. She noticed me standing behind a wall post. I was hiding, hoping she wouldn't see me.

"Marvin!" she yelled out. She was headed towards the exit, so I walked over to her to say a quick hello and goodbye. "You have a case here today?" she asked.

"Yes."

"What client? Is it the Alvarez family? I saw them. They entered the court right before me," she continued.

"No, not the Alvarez family. It's a new family, and we just finished. In fact, I was on my way out. I can walk you out if you're leaving. "

"Okay," she said.

As we entered the elevator, I prayed my real case was not called as I had faked exiting the court with my coworker. When we got downstairs, I made up an excuse that I had left my computer bag upstairs and told her she didn't have to wait.

"No worries. I can wait."

"No, it's okay. I need to use the restroom and then talk with the family's attorney once more. I forgot to ask about the next date."

"Okay. I'll see you back at the office."

Exhausting. I was glad we were finally at the finish line.

As Katherine took the stand, the court officer reminded her she was still under oath. I looked directly at her. Even though my seat was positioned in line with the witness chair, she didn't look in my direction.

Her attorney began the questioning. "Please tell me about your relationship with the father. When did it begin?"

"We met around June 2008."

"To your knowledge, was the father married at the time?"

"Objection, relevance," my attorney called out.

"Your Honor, I'm trying to establish a clear understanding of the parents' relationship just prior to the child's birth."

"Overruled. The witness may answer."

"No, I didn't know he was married. He told me that much later."

My attorney leaned over to me and whispered, "Time to buckle up. This testimony is going to be a bumpy ride."

One hour into her testimony and my attorney was right. Katherine didn't hold back one iota. She testified that I was a "cheater and despicable liar." She doubled down on her false, unsubstantiated allegations, especially the most recent ones involving Anyanwu. She said I used my "considerable influence" over OCFS to have the allegations dismissed as unfounded and that I somehow had manipulated the police to not pursue charges against Anyanwu and me. She concluded her testimony by saying I was a bad father, I never really loved our child or her, I never wanted our child in my life, and the only reason I was taking care of Kisha now was so she wouldn't have to go into foster care or so I wouldn't have to pay Katherine child support.

There was some truth in her last statement. I wasn't ready for full-time care of Kisha. I foolishly didn't think Katherine would get pregnant. I had told her I loved her, but I realized our relationship was soiled with codependency. And no, I didn't want my daughter to go into foster care. I had never thought about court-ordered child support. I had been already giving Katherine about four hundred dollars monthly for Kisha's care once I had left the home. That was the extent of the truth in her testimony. I love my daughter very much and will always love her.

At that moment, I wished I were somewhere else singing show tunes with my daughter. Unfortunately, I was at court listening to Katherine berate my character, spinning fabricated yarns and yarns about how horrible a man her once "loving fiancé'" had now become.

It's tragic how these sad moments can overshadow and erase most if not all positive moments in a couple's life. Truth is, even as I listened to Katherine denigrate my name, I realized that I didn't hate her. I was extremely angry, hurt, and very disappointed Katherine had chosen to manage our parenting issues in this manner, but I didn't hate her. I had made the decision to not hate her early on in our custody process. I don't remember consciously making the decision. I simply determined that no matter how bad it got between us, I wouldn't allow myself to speak ill of Katherine around our daughter. To help accomplish this, I didn't allow my friends and family to speak foully about Katherine around me. I couldn't bathe my mind in negative talk about Katherine without being affected. Of course, I didn't prevent my family and friends from expressing their dismay and concern about this situation. However, if the dismay and/or concern turned dark, I'd either change or end the subject. Without realizing it, this practice helped me to shield hatred from entering my heart. So as much as I could have hated Katherine, at that moment I didn't.

As difficult as it was for me to listen to Katherine wildly exaggerate the truth, it was equally as challenging for her upon cross-examination. All three attorneys—my lawyer, my daughter's attorney, and OCFS's court representative—didn't pull any punches. They hurled one difficult question after the next. With each inquiry, Katherine's replies called into question the validity of many, if not all, of the things she'd said during her direct testimony. Her attorney attempted to intercept as many questions as she could with her objections, but the judge allowed most of the questions. This continued for at least one hour. Out of all the witnesses, Katherine was on the stand the longest. She was visibly irritated and appeared physically drained. Surprisingly, her attorney didn't call for a break. Perhaps she wanted this to be over as well.

My attorney asked the final question. "If you had it your way, what would you do?"

"You mean if I could determine the outcome of this case?"

"Yes," he said.

"Well, based upon the fact that the father has a history of abuse towards my daughter, I'd give myself full physical and legal custody, and give the father monitored visits once weekly."

All attorneys rested after Katherine's final statement. The courtroom fell silent. Katherine didn't realize she had possibly dug her own grave with that last response.

The judge eventually spoke. "I've listened intently to the witness testimonies over the past six months, including both the father's and your testimony," she addressed the mother. "I can confidently say to you I found 90 percent of what you said to not be credible."

"Did you say credible, Your Honor?" Katherine's attorney asked.

"No, I said *not* credible," the judge said. To Katherine, she said, "You were irritated, unsure, and nonlucid during much of your testimony. You contradicted yourself several times, and many times I felt you were making things up as your testimony proceeded. Most of what you said could be directly refuted by the testimony of your own witnesses and the child's interviews. I contrasted this with the father's testimony. He presented calmly and patiently. Additionally, his testimony was in complete alignment with what many other professionals have reported of this case, including OCFS workers, police officers, the child's schoolteachers, and even some of the witnesses called in your defense.

"It is the opinion of this court that OCFS's allegations that the mother emotionally abused her child, including coaching the child to lie against her father and interrogating the child after visitations, are in fact true and accurate. As a result, the child shall be placed in the father's full-time care, with the father having full physical and legal custody. The mother shall have visits three times weekly—Monday, Wednesday, and Friday and every other weekend. I will leave it up to the father whether to have the child continue therapy at this time. I recommend she does for a time, and when appropriate, the mother and child must attend conjoint therapy."

"Your Honor, what about the school stay-away order?" my daughter's attorney asked. "The stay-away order is hereby removed, the stay-away order for the father's residence remains," the judge replied. She continued, "Once the mother and daughter engage in an appropriate amount of therapy as determined by the respective therapists and family court judge, it will be based upon the discretion of the family court judge to alter any of these orders. If there are no further questions or comments, this concludes this court hearing."

And with those words, it was finally over. I talked a moment with my attorney and exited the court quickly afterwards. I went to my van and sat quietly for a long while. Then it hit me like a rush of wind. I felt weak for a moment: no more dependency court, no more OCFS, and most importantly with the closing of this case, my daughter was no longer a ward of the state. Tears of joy collected in my eyes. I didn't try to hold them back.

I let them stream down my face as I thanked God repeatedly.

After school, I picked Kisha up and took her to one of her favorite restaurants. Anyanwu and her son joined us. We had a wonderful time eating, laughing, and enjoying one another's company. Even though Kisha and Anyanwu's son didn't know why we had chosen a school night to go out for dinner, it was a great way to celebrate without calling it a celebration. Later that night, my daughter and I sat in the middle of our living room. There was so much I wished I could share with her about the journey I'd endured, but she wouldn't understand. Truthfully, if she could have understood, I would have probably decided not to burden her thoughts with it. Of course, there were things she already knew, such as that she could see her mother only on certain days. I knew I had to explain to Kisha that this visitation schedule would continue until the court said otherwise. But for now, at this moment, the most important thing was that she was safe and happy.

CHAPTER TWELVE

LESSONS LEARNED

The nuances of my situation can't be neatly packaged into this brief narrative. Like many parents who have gone through this journey, I experienced a great deal that, if explained in detail, would read as long as *War and Peace*. However, there were specific lessons I learned, lessons I now cherish and that help guide my parenting life.

NEVER GIVE UP

There were times during this process when I seriously considered throwing in the towel. I thought my journey to fatherhood would be too difficult a challenge to overcome. The times I was most locked into this mindset were when I isolated myself from those individuals who loved me most. In seclusion, my mind drowned in harmful thinking. These damaging thoughts were able to flourish because there were no intervening voices to say, "Hey, everything will be okay. Don't give up." Isolation provided false comfort and gave me the space during investigations and numerous court hearings to hide and feel sorry for myself.

I'm thankful my family and loved ones didn't let me stay too long in such a debilitating place. I'm glad I found a group of men who shared my journey and held one another accountable while simultaneously inspiring one another to be the best fathers we could be despite our monumental challenges. Today when I look upon my daughter's smiling eyes, I'm so happy I never gave up believing she was worth the struggle.

DON'T OPERATE OUT OF FEAR

What stopped me from going to court sooner than I did was fear of the outcome. During my conversations with fathers, I heard a common theme: "Courts favor the mother." For many decades, this was definitely the case. During those times, the prevailing sentiment in most courts throughout the country was that the mother was the most appropriate primary caregiver. This sentiment guided the decision-making of many courts and contributed to the creation of the "weekend dad." Many fathers were relegated to a partial relationship with their children. We accepted this narrative and didn't fight for our rights in family court, or we avoided family court altogether. Over the past several years, with the assistance of advocacy groups such as Project Fatherhood and individual fathers brave enough to stand up for their equal parental rights, courts have started to recognize the importance of shared custody and the value of allowing children to experience more time around their fathers beyond weekends.

I discovered that facing my fear of family court could lead to a favorable and, more importantly, balanced court decision.

There were times during my court process when fear consumed and exhausted me. One day while sitting in my living room, hiding from my friends and family, I realized my biggest fear was that I'd one day wake up after fighting a tremendous battle in court, having expended infinite amounts of time, energy, and resources, and still end up losing all rights to be around my daughter. I now know that even though courts still favor the mother's role in custody matters, the importance of the father's role in his children's life is beginning to be appreciated by judges nationwide. I encourage fathers to embrace the value of their role in their child's life and to never allow fear let anyone, not even themselves, stop them from being a present and dutiful father.

REMAIN ACCOUNTABLE

A beautiful aspect of the fatherhood group, I attended, was that each participant was charged with the responsibility of keeping the other participants accountable. This was a valuable feature of the meeting because the tendency to blame others for your circumstances is easy to fall into. Accountability is a constant reminder in your mind's ear that even though the road most traveled is convenient (blaming others), you should keep going on the road less traveled and not place full blame for the adverse situations you face on your child's mother, OCFS, or the courts.

The road less traveled will cause you to stop and examine your situation from a fair and honest perspective. The road less traveled won't allow you to transfer all the blame and take none for yourself. Being an accountable traveler entails engaging in a lot of self-reflection. Remaining accountable is an antidote for self-pity, false pride, and self-aggrandizement. Personally, the moment I embraced the concept of self-accountability was the moment I could forgive myself for the wrongs I had committed in my relationship with my child's mother and other failed relationships, and work on not repeating those counterproductive practices in my relationships moving forth.

PRACTICE FORGIVENESS

This lesson is difficult. How does one forgive a person who actively works to ruin his or her own life and the lives of those he or she loves?

The road to forgiveness is littered with many barriers, primarily a lack of self-accountability and hatred. We already discussed accountability, and we'll discuss hatred in more detail shortly. The word *practice* is the focus here. Forgiveness isn't an automatic action. It requires conscious effort. When someone deeply injuries you, physically or emotionally, forgiveness becomes less of an option in your thoughts. That's why one must practice forgiveness routinely to achieve any level of success.

What does practice entail? Through my journey, I found that practicing forgiveness requires me to be vigilant about not letting hatred soil my thoughts. Hatred is a cancerous disease, and if allowed to flourish, it will negatively affect your thoughts and actions. Forgiveness can free you from the physical and spiritual trappings of a negative relationship with another or yourself. In order to move on from a negative relationship, we must forgive ourselves for the way we behaved and the choices we made while in contaminated relationship environments. Sometimes this includes forgiving yourself for hurting another or allowing someone to lessen your value as a human being. Practicing forgiveness isn't an easy task, but doing it will free your heart to be happier and to love more abundantly.

GUARD AGAINST RIGID PARENTING

A prolific music producer once told me that in order for music producers to remain relevant, they can't become rigid. He elaborated, "When a music producer gets fixed to a certain sound or style of music, they close their mind to the possibility of hearing sounds that, even though different from what they are accustomed to, could be the next big hit."

I never imagined I'd one day apply his advice to parenting. However, I have learned effective parenting can't happen in a static environment. Parental methods and strategies that worked for our parents or grandparents may not be useful tools for the present generation. Rigid parenting is the refusal to accept that you as the parent don't have a monopoly on all good parenting ideas and should be open to learning what works best for the child before you. We must parent from current realities, utilizing all the tools at our disposal, and when there aren't tools at our immediate disposal, we need to identify where and how to obtain those tools.

There's comfort in what we know. This includes parenting methodologies. For instance, when our children want to listen to a song on the radio, don't criticize it as trash or not real music. Listen to the song with your child and ask nonjudgmental questions to discover why your child likes it. This can create the opportunity to fit in a point or two about whether the song is socially responsible. When we feel the tendency to drift into a judgmental state of mind, we must resist.

One way I remember is to reflect on the words of Khalil Gibran when he admonished parents to not think of children as property but as temporary souls we are only meant to responsibly guide, not to own.

AN OUNCE OF PREVENTION IS WORTH A POUND OF CURE

For years I'd enter into relationships recklessly. I didn't use emotional or sometimes even physical protection (condoms), and I never thought about the consequences that could result from my actions. My priority was how my partners made *me* feel, emotionally, mentally, and physically. I didn't think deeply about whether I was emotionally or mentally compatible with my past partners, including my ex-wife or child's mother. I wanted them to view me as attractive and intelligent. I needed their validation to feel good about myself. This relationship pathology guided me through physical relationships, one after the next. I didn't realize it at the time. It took years of broken relationships, a failed marriage, a beautiful child born out of wedlock, horrific court battles, and meeting my current wife to come to this understanding.

Today I understand the importance of not choosing a partner from a place of insecurity or emotional deficit. Yes, it's important for your partner to contribute positively to your overall mental and physical well-being, but they can't be solely responsible for your happiness. Sex can be an important part of a romantic relationship, and the bottom line is people are going to have sex. But what I understand now is that before entering into a relationship, short term or long term, sexual or romantic, it's important to consider whether or not the person is someone who can help you build a healthy, lasting future. This will require compatibility and constant self-accountability. If the person is not compatible to build a future with, it still requires honesty, self-discipline, and clear communication on your part. Most important, if a child becomes involved in the relationship, would the other person or you commit to contributing positively to the child's life? Would you and the other person be a positive example of a healthy relationship for the child?

Until you're mature and stable enough to handle the wonderful complexities relationships bring, especially child-rearing, pause and get to know your partner in a nonsexual way, or at the very least get in the habit of wearing protection each and every time you have sex. Spare yourself and others the pain of my experience.

CHOOSE LOVE OVER HATE

Lennon and McCartney penned the popular tune "All You Need Is Love," a great song with a powerful message. Through my situation, I've come to firmly believe hatred is a cancer and love is the cure.

My immense love for my daughter is one of the reasons I couldn't justify hate in my heart throughout my journey. My love for her wouldn't allow my intense negative feelings to surface or flourish within me. If those negative feelings flourished and subsequently emerged, hatred wouldn't be too far behind. Operating from a place of hatred would have prevented me from doing the things I needed to do to ensure my daughter remained free of the foster care system. Hatred would have placed me in a deeply dark place: a place where anger and false pride flourished. Remaining calm in court and through OCFS interviews would have been virtually impossible. Love buoyed me when the dangerous waters of self-pity, anger, fear, and doubt nearly drowned my soul.

EPILOGUE

In the four years since the conclusion of dependency court, I have continued to have full legal and physical custody of my daughter. Kisha's visits with her mother are still three times weekly and every other weekend, and Kisha attended individual therapy sessions. I mention this because most children in my daughter's position never get a safe place to process their feelings about the tumultuous situations they've endured, and this void can lead to disastrous outcomes later in their lives such as drug abuse, gang involvement, or sometimes suicide. If you have a situation similar to mine, I urge you to consider providing your child with that safe space.

Anyanwu and I have been happily married for three years now, and I'm a stepdad to her son. I could write an entire book on that subject alone. I'm learning to be a good stepdad. You have to leave your ego at the door. As a stepparent, you try hard to get your stepchildren to love you, or maybe just to like you. These efforts are often met with resistance or indifference. Either reaction can bruise a fragile ego. Leaving ego at the proverbial door helps to temper your expectations or to not have any expectations for reciprocal action or positive reaction when you do something kind or helpful for your stepchild.

Second, don't overstep your role, no pun intended. A stepparent isn't the biological parent and shouldn't attempt to be so, even if the biological parent isn't present full time or at all. Be yourself and the best support for the biological parent you can possibly be. Allow the relationship that develops between you and the stepchild to be unique and natural.

Anyanwu and I were married in a beautiful Sunday afternoon ceremony with family and friends there to enjoy the precious moment with us. It remains one of the happiest days of my life. It was an outdoor ceremony with a magnificent view of New York City. The view was beautiful, but not nearly as breathtaking as Anyanwu was that day. Many family members and close friends were able to attend. My first cousin performed the ceremony, and my daughter was the flower girl. Maybe one day she will write a book about her journey, a guide to other children like her, on how to continue being happy during a tumultuous tornado.

My life isn't perfect. I'm learning through trial and error how to be a better person. Negotiating matters with Katherine remains a challenge, one that will require vigilance and forgiveness for a long time. Nonetheless, when I sit at home and look around at my little family—my beautiful and talented wife, my wonderfully weird daughter, and my precocious stepson—I can honestly say I'm happy and grateful that my journey led me here.

Follow Mark Winkler

Instagram @fatherhood_circle

Facebook @fatherhood_circle

Website: https://markrwinkler.com/